FOOD OF THE SOUTHERN FORESTS

PRODUCE, PORTRAITS & RECIPES

SOPHIE ZALOKAR

Photography by Craig Kinder

For Ivan + Leslie
From one kitchen at the edge of
the world to another, happy
cooking!   Sophie Zalokar

Jan. 2023

First published in 2014 by
UWA Publishing
Crawley, Western Australia 6009
www.uwap.uwa.edu.au
UWA Publishing is a division of The University of Western Australia.

 THE UNIVERSITY OF
WESTERN AUSTRALIA

Author: Zalokar, Sophie, 1967- author.

Title: Food of the southern forests : produce, portraits
and recipes / Sophie Zalokar ; photography by Craig Kinder.

ISBN: 9781742585512 (hardback)

Notes: Includes bibliographical references and index.

Subjects: Cooking — Western Australia, Southwest.
Western Australia, Southwest — Social life and customs.

Other Authors/Contributors:
Kinder, Craig, photographer.

Dewey Number: 641.5099412

Designed by Xou Creative
Printed by Imago

CONTENTS

CONTENTS (CONTINUED)

For the primary producers of the Southern Forests region, with gratitude.

May you see the returns you justly deserve.

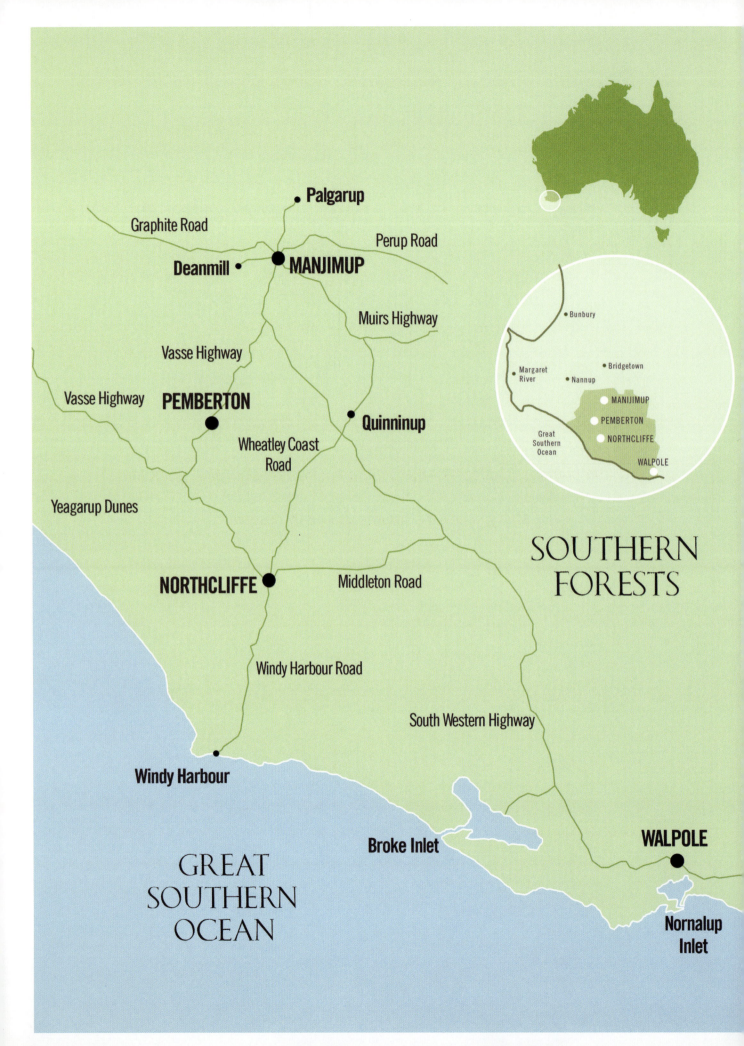

Palgarup

Graphite Road

Perup Road

Deanmill ● **MANJIMUP**

Muirs Highway

Vasse Highway

Vasse Highway

PEMBERTON

● **Quinninup**

Wheatley Coast Road

Yeagarup Dunes

NORTHCLIFFE

Middleton Road

Windy Harbour Road

South Western Highway

Windy Harbour

Broke Inlet

WALPOLE

GREAT SOUTHERN OCEAN

Nornalup Inlet

SOUTHERN FORESTS

● Bunbury

● Margaret River

● Bridgetown

● Nannup

○ MANIJIMUP

○ PEMBERTON

○ NORTHCLIFFE

Great Southern Ocean

○ WALPOLE

PREFACE

There's been a great deal of talk around the growing, sourcing, preparation and enjoyment of fresh food over the last few years.

We're starting to recognise the impact food has on our health and well-being, and to value the enormous role it now plays in our daily social lives. We're also starting to think about the long-ignored but inherent environmental costs, questioning where and how fresh produce is grown and sourced, and seeking a greater connection with our local food and those who grow it.

Mass media, social media and now the smart-phone app phenomenon are introducing us to both the artisanal and the larger growers and producers of food, as part of a less commercialised and more authentic tourism experience.

You may not be familiar with the name Southern Forests or know where it is, but if you live anywhere in Western Australia you've probably been eating fresh food grown in this region all your life and not known it was produced here. If you've visited this region from interstate or overseas, your memories are more than likely dominated by the majestic trees rather than what's grown in the fields amongst them.

If, however, you're a bit of a foodie and have either read about us or come along to one of the region's food festivals, there's a good chance you may associate Manjimup with cherries, apples and now truffles, Pemberton with marron, trout and now avocados, Northcliffe with milk and cream or Walpole with beef.

As a cook in this region interested in what's grown here and who grows it, I've had the great privilege of getting to know not only the producers mentioned in this book, but many others who've taken that optimistically calculated risk of being a grower or food producer, recognising the culinary potential of this incredible place.

The common denominators between them all are a genuine sense of pride in their work, family traditions, community, spirit and an understanding of the value of the region's temperate climate, clean air, abundant water and deep soils that are capable of the fertility required for food production.

As a tourism operator in this region, I have heard the lament time and time again, 'I wish we had more time and ways of seeing and experiencing what we've only just found out is here.' The magnificent karri forests have long been the sole tourism focus and reason for visiting, but now the Southern Forests is seeking to develop a culinary tourism experience that goes beyond the restaurant cellar door and back along our winding forests tracks to where it all begins – the farm gate.

It's an exciting future that we wish to develop and share with you when you visit the region, and one we'll continue to offer you through the fresh food on your table: a genuine and authentic taste of the Southern Forests region.

INTRODUCTION

The Southern Forests region is in the lower south-west of Western Australia, approximately 300 km south of Perth. It's an extraordinarily beautiful place. The majestic native karri forests, with trees amongst the tallest in the world, scrape abundant skies and edge lush pastures, orchards and vineyards, while deep through the valleys, serene waterways roll with a primal rhythm and descend towards an ancient and wild coastal rim.

It is a prehistoric and richly bio-diverse area in Australia's largest state, with an agriculturally dependent economy that has the physical and geographical capacity to grow far more fresh food than meets the current needs of Western Australia – and well beyond.

The first caretakers of the Southern Forests region were the Aboriginal Nyungar / Murrum people, who are estimated to have lived in the region for some 30,000 years. Sadly, very little has been recorded by early settlers or evidence left of their presence, partly because they cared for the land in a way that left no permanent scarring. The significant history and cultural heritage of the first truly sustainable lifestyle leaders has unfortunately taken some time to be recognised.

Part of their cultural legacy, however, is represented in the naming of several places. 'Up' on the ending of a place name means a 'place of…' that is usually located near water. Manjimup takes its name from Manjimup Brook – where the highly valued edible root of the 'Manjin' rush was found, which was roasted and pounded to make a kind of cake.

The official boundaries of the Southern Forests are marked out as the municipality of the Shire of Manjimup, but its Blackwood River Valley neighbours in the west and north and Great Southern neighbours in the south and east are valued good friends.

Around 10,000 locals are spread over the four main towns of Manjimup, Pemberton, Northcliffe and Walpole together with smaller settlements, communities and outlying farming properties. A quarter of the population is involved in agriculture, forestry and fishing; many of them are also dedicated to their local football clubs, which have a long, colourful history of friendly rivalry.

Those who come from families who pioneered the local agriculture, timber, viticulture and tourism industries over a 150-year span possess the same resilient will to survive and sense of self-determination as their grandparents and, in some cases, great-grandparents before them.

Wilderness, National Parks, State Forests or Reserves make up 85% of the region's 7,000 square kilometres. If you, like me, can't imagine this measurement of land, it's best described as hours and hours of spectacular scenic driving, the best of which can be experienced year-round off the sealed roads, guided by local knowledge.

Remarkably, over fifty different types of fresh produce are cultivated, harvested, ranged and caught from either the natural waterways or 140 km of pristine coastline and over 80,000 hectares of prime agricultural land. The gross, and increasing, agricultural value of this produce is $127 million each year.

This book aims to introduce you to some of the produce grown in this unique place, the people who grow it and a little of the wonderful migrant food heritage, together with recipes I've developed that are examples of how this produce can be prepared and enjoyed.

It represents only a fraction of what comes from the Southern Forests, but it attempts to take you on a virtual tour around the region, visiting farms and talking with growers who've all been incredibly generous with their time, knowledge and willingness to allow us into their working lives.

After seeing the quality and diversity displayed through these pages, I'm sure you'll agree that the Southern Forests has not only earned its reputation as the food bowl of Western Australia, but that its ability to grow so many different and high-quality foods is something very special, and very worth seeking out for yourself.

APPLES, PEARS & QUINCES

NEWTON ORCHARDS OF MANJIMUP & VALLEYVIEW ORGANICS

The Southern Forests is the largest apple-growing region in Western Australia. Of the many pome fruit orchards planted in Manjimup and Pemberton, two alone produce 60% of WA's total annual apple harvest. Newton Orchards of Manjimup is one of them and feels privileged to be.

In 1929, brothers George and Harold Newton, who were 16 and 15 years old at the time, travelled to Manjimup by way of the Margaret River area. They had arrived in Australia from England in 1927 via the popular sponsored £10 scheme for rural labour. They started out with 100 acres, which they cleared and planted with vegetable and then fruit crops.

Perhaps offering some comfort at the time, George and Harold were not alone in experiencing the hard graft needed to clear the land of the region's behemoth trees. Joseph Johnson had also been clearing land for fruit trees as the first settler to establish apple growing on a commercial basis near Manjimup.

A report in the *Journal of Agriculture, Western Australia* in 1904 by horticultural inspector George W. Wickens describes Johnson's effective clearing of land: 'As an example of pluck and energy, I think the following undertaking is hard to beat: Mr Johnson took delivery on 20 July last of 300 fruit trees (enough to plant 3 acres) and had to clear off green timber, fence and plough the land before he could plant a single tree. The work was all done single handed, with the exception of a man and team for three days dragging logs together. The fruit trees were planted and the ground ploughed and fenced by 10 September. Anyone who has seen the country referred to will realize the amount of work entailed in getting the trees planted.'

By 1930, the agricultural produce of the area included around 960 tonnes of apples – which would have given George and Harold great hope for the future, despite the hard and lean years of the Great Depression over the following decade. Throughout the 1950s the then-trading Newton Brothers Orchards began developing its reputation for premium quality fruit, innovative growing methods and cool storage that the Giblett family has consciously worked hard to continue.

All of George's six children worked in the orchards and packhouse; however, since the early 1990s his son-in-law Harvey Giblett has owned and operated Newton Orchards. 'Dad's always had a very quiet unassuming modesty about his role, regarded himself as a caretaker of the land. He genuinely searches for outstanding quality and feels privileged to be able to produce a healthy product for so many West Australians,' his daughter Nicole describes her father.

In the spirit of George and Harold's drive and innovation, the Giblett family together with Nicole's partner, Paul Good, who manages the finance and export development areas of the business, recently launched the ValleyView Organics brand that includes Pink Lady, Royal Gala, Fuji, Granny Smith and various other heritage apple and quince varieties.

Their Newton Orchards brand conventionally grows Sundowner, Pink Lady, Red Delicious, Fuji, Granny Smith, Royal Gala and the newer Greenstar, Kanzi and Jazz varieties. A leading UK importer has advised that they have one of the shortest chemical lists of a non-organic grower, more than meeting the strictest standards in the world.

Despite downscaling their numbers of pears in recent years, Newton Orchards also produces the West-Australian developed Goldrush, Bartlett and Packham varieties. In smaller, more niche amounts, they also grow the Perup Pride and Golden Delicious apples, several varieties of cherries, Satsuma and Ebony Sun plums and Kinross apricots – primarily available direct through the Manjimup Farmers Market.

Most of their 5,500 tonne per year harvest is supplied into the major supermarket chains and independent stores throughout Western Australia. This means West Australians have quite likely been enjoying Newton Orchards apples for years. Approximately 10-15% of their production goes into the eastern states market and a further 5-10% to export.

Of all the apple varieties that Newton Orchards and others have grown in the Southern Forests, the Pink Lady has had the most significance in terms of its reach and favourability around the world.

In the early 1970s John Cripps crossed a Golden Delicious with a Lady Williams and developed the apple variety Cripps Pink. With a distinctive pink blush, fabulous crunch and fizzy sweet flavour, it can be enjoyed fresh and successfully cooked as it retains its structure and flavour when heated. 'Unusually, the Pink Lady is one of the few varieties not best eaten straight from the tree. The flavour profile benefits from cool storage as the fruit's natural acids drop away with time and integrate better with the flavour profile,' explains Nicole.

The Pink Lady® brand apple was trademarked and specific quality standards set by Apple and Pear Australia Limited for apples of the Cripps Pink variety. As a result, it's now registered in more than 70 countries and grown around the world.

Despite its universal appeal, however, it is a little known fact that it was first commercially grown in Manjimup. In the 2014 apple season, the Pink Lady's 40 years of commercial existence was celebrated at events in Manjimup. 'We wish to commemorate the origins and history of the Pink Lady, recognising the attributes of this unique variety which are lost when this apple is viewed as a generic global commodity,' Nicole explains.

The original tree still lives at the Horticulture Research Centre in Manjimup, with a plaque commemorating this variety that has become one of the great success stories of the fruit industry.

Along with raising a fourth generation while driving their collective brands of quality fruit forward, Nicole played an establishing role in the formation of the Southern Forests Food Council as the elected inaugural vice-chairperson.

Asked about her hopes for their future and other growers in the region, Nicole replies, 'I just want to see an incremental 5-10% increase in return, which will make businesses just that bit more sustainable and help towards better renumerating cutting edge growers who take care and great pride in what they do. Our outlook is positive with Asia on our doorstep, but we'd love our customers to develop more realistic expectations of natural products, understanding that discarding produce with the slightest cosmetic imperfections and year-round availability of every fruit and veg from across the globe are just not sustainable practices.'

Just as George and Harold were digging and planting alongside others and with the legacy of Harvey Giblett's unwavering integrity, the Newton Orchards and ValleyView Organics brands are quietly moving forward, strengthening and growing within a community of producers who continue to pioneer new produce in the Southern Forests.

APPLE TRADITIONALLY accompanies pork dishes; however, it is equally delicious with chicken when accompanied by a few other compatible flavours. Apple saba is a thick syrup made from concentrated apple must and an Italian condiment; it's used similarly to the best balsamic vinegars.

ROAST CHICKEN, APPLE, LEEK, JUNIPER, SPECK, BAY LEAF & APPLE SABA

1 ½ tbsp juniper berries

1 x 2 kg free-range chicken

salt flakes & freshly cracked black pepper

6 fresh bay leaves

150 g speck or pancetta, sliced

1 ½ cups apple cider or apple juice

30 g butter

2 med leeks, the white section thickly sliced

3 Pink Lady apples, cored & thickly cross-section sliced

1 tbsp apple saba or Balsamic vinegar

SERVES 4

Preheat oven to 220 °C. Coarsely crush the juniper berries in a mortar and pestle. Generously season the chicken with salt flakes, cracked black pepper and 1 tablespoon of juniper berries including the cavity. Place two bay leaves inside the chicken and then evenly overlap the speck slices over the top of the chicken to cover. Sit the chicken on top of the remaining four bay leaves on the bottom of a heavy-based roasting dish. Pour in 1 cup of the apple cider before roasting in the oven for 15 minutes. Reduce the temperature to 180 °C and cook for 1 ½ hours.

Transfer the chicken to a plate and loosely cover with foil to rest for 15 minutes. Pour off the roasting juices through a sieve into a small bowl, scraping the bottom of the pan as clean as possible. Reserve the bay leaves for garnish.

Gently heat the roasting dish with the butter and sauté the leek with the remaining ½ tablespoon of juniper berries until the leek has softened. Deglaze with the remaining ½ cup apple cider and reserved roasting juices. Bring to a simmer before adding the apple slices. Simmer until the apple has just started to soften and then reserve to the side. Reduce the liquid until a syrupy consistency before stirring through the apple saba.

Remove the speck slices and roughly chop into bite-sized pieces. Carve the chicken and arrange on a preheated platter together with the apple slices and speck. Spoon over the sauce and garnish with the reserved bay leaves before serving.

BE PREPARED to loose control when tasting the smoky lapsang souchong caramel for the first time, especially when combined with this moist, rich marzipan cake full of fresh pear and scented with cardamom.

PEAR & CARDAMOM MARZIPAN CAKE WITH LAPSANG SOUCHONG CARAMEL CREAM

Marzipan

250 g almond meal
200 g icing sugar
1 tsp lemon juice
½ tsp almond extract
2 tbsp water

Lapsang Souchong Caramel Cream

300 ml Bannister Downs Whipping Cream
2 ½ tsp loose leaf lapsang souchong tea
1 tsp vanilla extract
1 cup white sugar
2 tbsp water
100 g unsalted butter
½ tsp salt

Pear & Cardamom Marzipan Cake

250 g unsalted butter, softened
250 g marzipan, softened
150 g caster sugar
¼ tsp almond extract
¼ tsp vanilla extract
6 free-range eggs
150 g self-raising flour
100 g almond meal
1 tsp ground cardamom
2 cups diced ripe pears

SERVES 12

MARZIPAN

Blend all of the ingredients together in a food processor until they just start forming a mass. Transfer to a clean work surface and knead until smooth. Roll into a thick log shape, cover with plastic wrap and refrigerate until needed. Left over marzipan can be frozen for future use.

LAPSANG SOUCHONG CARAMEL CREAM

Heat cream until just about simmering, remove from heat and stir through the tea leaves, cover and leave for 30 minutes. Strain into a measuring jug and stir through the vanilla. Heat the sugar with water in a heavy-based saucepan, gently moving the saucepan to evenly melt. Boil until a deep golden colour, remove from the heat and then quickly add the butter in tablespoon amounts. Add the salt and then carefully pour in the cream. Bring back to the boil for 2 to 3 minutes and then transfer into a heatproof bowl. Allow to cool and then refrigerate.

PEAR & CARDAMOM MARZIPAN CAKE

Preheat oven to 170 °C. Butter and lightly flour a bundt cake tin. Beat the butter and marzipan with the sugar until creamy. Add almond and vanilla extracts and then incorporate the eggs one at a time. Mix in the flour, almond meal and cardamom until well combined. Fold through the diced pears before scraping into the prepared tin.

Bake for 40 to 45 minutes, until the cake looks golden and cooked. Leave to cool for 10 minutes in the tin before turning out. Serve with the Lapsong Souchong Caramel Cream poured over the top.

QUINCES HAVE a bold perfumed flavour when cooked that matches beautifully with chocolate. Inspired by Maggie Beer's Chocolate, Quince and Almond Tart, this dessert takes a further luscious-leap with a silky chocolate ganache filling flavoured with liquorice. Given its richness, serve in sliver portions!

CHOCOLATE, QUINCE & LIQUORICE TART

Pastry

190 g unsalted butter, softened
190 g caster sugar
1 tsp vanilla extract
225 g plain flour
75 g (+ extra) Dutch cocoa powder

Filling

4 small or 1 kg fresh quinces, peeled, quartered & cored
1 litre apple juice
300 g caster sugar
2 lemons, juiced
300 ml cream
380 g dark chocolate
¼ tsp aniseed essence
100 g soft liquorice, cut into small pieces

SERVES 4

To poach the quinces, heat the apple juice, caster sugar and lemon juice in a wide, heavy-based saucepan, stirring to dissolve the sugar. Place the quince quarters in the syrup, adding water if necessary to ensure the liquid covers the fruit, and cover with a piece of baking paper. Weigh the quinces down with a plate to keep them submerged and simmer very gently with the lid on for 1 hour, until the quinces have softened. Remove the lid, plate and baking paper and keep simmering for a further 30 minutes to reduce the syrup and deepen the pale pink colour of the quinces. Remove the quinces with a slotted spoon and allow to cool before slicing thickly.

To make the pastry, cream the butter and sugar in an electric mixer until pale and then beat in the vanilla extract. Sift the flour and cocoa together and blend into the butter mixture until just incorporated. Grease a 24 cm loose-bottomed tart tin and gently press the dough over the base and up the sides to create an even tart base. Rest in the refrigerator for a minimum of one hour. Preheat oven to 180 °C and bake the pastry base for 10 to 15 minutes. If the sides collapse, press the pastry gently back into place while still warm. Leave to cool.

To make the filling, bring the cream to a gentle simmer in a saucepan, turn the heat off and add the chocolate. Stir until smooth and then stir through the aniseed essence. Leave to cool.

RECIPE CONTINUES >

Evenly lay the quince slices over the chocolate pastry base before scattering over the soft liquorice pieces. Pour over the chocolate filling and gently tap the tart to remove any air bubbles and ensure the filling is even. Allow to set on an even surface and in a cool place for 4 hours before serving.

APRICOTS, PEACHES, PLUMS & NECTARINES

THE GUADAGNINO FAMILY

Until recently, brother and sister Ray and Fran worked together at their family business, Alf's Continental Store in Manjimup. Walking in on a lively conversations between them was like listening to the essence of what food has meant to the Italian culture since time began: an enduring passion for fresh produce, prepared simply, and generously shared with others.

Their story, however, starts with their father, Alfonso Guadagnino. Sponsored by his uncle who was already in Western Australia, Alfonso left his wife Domenica in Calabria and travelled by ship from Messina in Sicily to Fremantle in 1951, arriving with a small suitcase and hopes of establishing a new life for his family.

He began working for Luisini Winery in the Wanneroo area, which was where many new Italian migrants to Western Australia had their start, then worked in various places including Geraldton as a chef. He made his way down south via Brunswick Junction and Harvey, hand digging potatoes and working in the dairies; in Bridgetown building fences and apple picking; and then eventually Manjimup where he worked on tobacco plantations and at the Jardee Mill.

Alfonso then bought a travelling green grocer business, to which he added many of the products in demand from the Italian community such as olive oil, dried pasta and legumes. Piling the back of his ute with seasonal produce, often bought from Macedonian migrants also in Manjimup, Alfonso travelled around to small communities in the region from the Shannon River in the south up the South Western Highway as far as Bunbury. There he would buy fresh fish to sell on his return to Manjimup. 'He used to tell us so many stories,' Fran recalls.

In the mid 60s, the family purchased 'Robbie's Corner', on the intersection of Giblett and Ipsen Street. Here, the travelling grocer for whom customer service was as important as the quality of his products found a permanent home, opening Alf's Continental Store in 1966. In 1970, the family purchased a 228 acre former potato farm on Seven Day Road to grow produce for the shop.

They started out with vegetables, then decided to concentrate on fruit, beginning with several varieties of apples and now growing many varieties of pome and stone fruits, tree nuts and chestnuts and prickly pears.

The much beloved Alfonso passed away in 1996. 'His dream was to make the farm a paradise, planting every type of fruit,' Fran explains. 'The boys have finished this dream for him.'

Today, Fran's husband, Tony Potito, together with his brothers in law Domenic and Ray, manage the orchards. As a result of the family choosing to focus on production rather than retail, Alf's Continental Store closed on the 31st May 2014; however, Fran, Domenic and Ray's sister Angelina and her husband Sarafino – who operate Balcatta Growers Fresh in Perth – will continue to stock and sell the family's fresh produce.

The Guadagnino family's story of tireless work to support their community and feed their families is similar to many; however, few continue today in the same way as their parents and grandparents before them. You can be sure this will include many more lively and passionate discussions about what to cook for dinner.

MACE IS a spice traditionally used for preparing terrines and pâtés but it also has a wonderful affinity with fresh apricots, adding an exotic perfumed quality to this dessert. If you can't find whole mace blades, use a quarter of the quantity in ground mace or ground nutmeg, with which it originally grows.

YOGHURT PISTACHIO CHEESECAKE WITH APRICOTS IN ORANGE BLOSSOM WATER, MACE & BAY LEAF SYRUP

Yoghurt Pistachio Cheesecake

150 g digestive biscuits

60 g almond meal

75 g unsalted butter, melted

4 titanium strength gelatine leaves

1 orange, the finely grated zest & juice of

500 g thick plain Greek yoghurt

500 ml crème fraîche

½ cup honey

1 tsp vanilla extract

Apricots In Orange Blossom Water, Mace & Bay Leaf Syrup

250 ml water

250 ml white wine

1 cup sugar

3 fresh bay leaves

1 tsp mace blades

8 – 10 ripe apricots, halved

1 tsp orange blossom water

To Serve

60 g pistachios, roughly chopped

SERVES 8

Line a 22 cm spring form baking tin with baking paper. Break the digestive biscuits up into small pieces and then blend with the almond meal in a food processor until fine but not clumping together. Transfer to a bowl and mix through the melted butter before pressing onto the base and halfway up the sides of the tin. Chill in the refrigerator while making the filling.

Soften the gelatine leaves in a bowl of cold water. Heat the orange juice in a small saucepan. Squeeze excess water out of the gelatine leaves before stirring through the hot orange juice to dissolve. Allow to cool. Mix the yoghurt, crème fraîche, honey, vanilla and orange zest together in a large bowl and then whisk through the orange juice mixture to combine. Pour this onto the biscuit base and return to the refrigerator for 4 to 5 hours to set.

Heat the water, wine, sugar, bay leaves and mace blades together. Gently simmer and occasionally stir for 5 minutes. Gently put the apricots in the syrup and return to a simmer. Turn the apricots over after 2 to 3 minutes. They need to soften but not lose their shape. Remove with a slotted spoon and reserve to the side. Boil the syrup until viscous and the flavour has intensified. Stir through the orange blossom water and then pour over the apricots. Place a piece of baking paper directly onto the surface and chill in the refrigerator.

Unmould the cheesecake, pile some of the apricots on top and scatter over the pistachios before serving with more of the apricots and syrup.

THE SPICED nectarines in this recipe add a lovely fruity tang that cuts through the creamy, rich and nutty flavours of tahini and peanut. Use them also on platters of preserved meats as an interesting alternative to olives.

GINGER-POACHED SHREDDED CHICKEN, PEANUT & SESAME SALAD WITH SPICED NECTARINES

Spiced Nectarines

10 sml nectarines,
halved & stones removed
450 ml apple cider vinegar
375 ml water
⅓ cup honey
3 tbsp white sugar
1 tsp salt
2 tsp whole allspice
2 tsp black peppercorns
1 tsp cloves
3 cinnamon sticks

Ginger-Poached Shredded Chicken

1.6 kg free-range chicken
1 cup rice wine vinegar
10 cloves garlic, peeled
180 g sliced fresh ginger
⅓ cup salt
½ sml Savoy cabbage, finely shredded
½ cup unsalted roasted peanuts,
roughly chopped
1 tsp toasted sesame seeds
1 tbsp fresh dill, roughly chopped
8 spiced nectarine halves, skins
discarded & flesh thickly sliced

Dressing

½ cup spiced nectarine syrup
2 tbsp hulled tahini
1 tbsp extra virgin olive oil
1 tsp lemon juice
sea salt flakes & freshly
cracked black pepper

SERVES 8

SPICED NECTARINES

Place the nectarine halves in a bowl. Bring the vinegar, water, honey, sugar, salt and spices to the boil, stirring until the sugar, honey and salt have dissolved. Pour over the nectarines and cover with a piece of baking paper directly on top. Leave to cool before refrigerating until ready to serve. Best for 2 weeks.

GINGER-POACHED SHREDDED CHICKEN

Place the chicken in a medium-sized stockpot. Cover with the rice wine vinegar, garlic, fresh ginger, salt and enough water to only just cover the chicken. Bring to a very gentle simmer and cook on low heat for 20 minutes. Turn the heat off and let the chicken sit in the pot until it's cool enough to handle. Take the meat off the bones, discarding the skin and bones and shred into bite-sized pieces. Cover and reserve to the side.

Make the dressing by simmering the spiced nectarine syrup in a small saucepan until the volume is reduced by half. Leave to cool before whisking in the tahini, extra virgin olive oil, lemon juice and seasoning. If needed, adjust with a little water until the consistency of pouring cream.

Toss the shredded chicken with the cabbage, peanuts, half the sesame seeds, half the dill and half the dressing together with a little seasoning. Serve with the remaining dressing drizzled on the top and garnished with the spiced nectarine slices, remaining peanuts, sesame seeds and dill.

A TARTINE is the French equivalent of the Italian bruschetta or English open sandwich. However you choose to describe them, the washed rind cheese and ham are great flavour partners with the very fruity pickled plums.

PICKLED PLUM, HAM, WASHED RIND CHEESE & RYE TARTINE

Pickled Plums

1 lemon
½ tsp whole cloves
1 x 2.5 cm piece ginger, julienne
600 ml apple cider vinegar
480 g sugar
1 kg blood plums

Ham, Washed Rind Cheese & Rye Tartine

4 thick slices rye sourdough, toasted
180 g washed rind cheese
1 sml handful curly endive or other bitter greens, washed
8 – 10 slices best-quality leg ham
4 pickled plum halves, sliced
freshly cracked black pepper
1 tsp fresh thyme leaves & flowers

SERVES 4

PICKLED PLUMS

Remove the zest from the lemon in wide strips using a peeler. Put the zest and all the remaining ingredients except the plums into a large saucepan and simmer for 10 minutes, stirring to ensure the sugar has dissolved.

Wash and dry the plums well, then cut them in half and remove the stones. Firmly layer and pack the plums into two warm 1 ½ litre rubber-sealed, clip-top sterilised jars. Pour over the hot syrup to cover the fruit, distributing the zest and cloves evenly between the jars as you do so. Immediately clip the rubber-sealed lids shut and then store to mature for a minimum of two weeks before using.

HAM, WASHED RIND CHEESE & RYE TARTINE

Thickly spread the washed rind cheese on the toasted rye sourdough. Place the curly endive and sliced ham on top and then the slices of pickled plum. Garnish with freshly cracked black pepper and fresh thyme.

PEACH LEAVES add a subtle almond flavour when used to infuse a custard base. It can be strengthened with additional almond extract as opposed to using more leaves, which can make the taste too bitter.

GRILLED PEACHES, HAZELNUT BISCOTTI, PEACH LEAF ICE CREAM & VIN SANTO

Hazelnut Biscotti

400 g plain flour
pinch salt
½ tsp baking powder
270 g caster sugar
½ tsp anise seeds
1 lemon, zest finely grated
1 lime, zest finely grated
100 g hazelnuts, roughly chopped
1 free-range egg yolk
2 free-range eggs
½ tsp vanilla extract

Peach Leaf Ice Cream

450 ml cream
200 ml full cream milk
¼ tsp salt
10 – 12 fresh peach leaves, unsprayed, rinsed and patted dry
6 large free-range egg yolks
½ cup sugar
2 – 3 drops almond extract (optional)

To Serve

4 tree-ripened peaches, halved & stoned
Vin Santo or other heavier-style dessert wine

SERVES 4

HAZELNUT BISCOTTI

Preheat oven to 180 °C. Combine the flour, salt, baking powder and anise seed. Add the zests and hazelnuts. Whisk the yolk and eggs with the vanilla and sugar until light and frothy and then fold in the dry ingredients. With wet hands, form into two logs on a baking paper–lined tray. Bake 30 minutes until the top springs back when lightly pressed. Leave to cool before cutting into 1 cm thick diagonal slices. Place on baking trays and return to the oven to bake for 20 to 30 minutes until just starting to colour. Cool on a wire rack.

PEACH LEAF ICE CREAM

Heat the cream, milk and salt together in a large saucepan until just simmering. Gently make tears along the edges of the peach leaves to help release the flavour and add them to the pan. When the mixture just begins to bubble around the edges, remove from the heat. Allow the leaves to steep for 15 minutes.

Whisk the egg yolks and sugar to combine. Reheat the cream until just simmering and slowly pour into the egg mixture while whisking. Return to the pan and cook carefully over low heat, stirring constantly, until it thickens and coats the back of a spatula.

Strain through a fine sieve into a bowl and leave in an ice-water bath, stirring occasionally until cool. Stir through the almond extract, cover with plastic wrap and refrigerate for 2 hours or overnight. Freeze in your ice cream machine according to manufacturer's instructions. RECIPE CONTINUES >

TO SERVE

Preheat an open barbecue grill or ridged grilling pan until very hot. Place the peaches cut side down on the grill and cook for 3 to 4 minutes until charred but with their shape retained. Serve together with a scoop of the Peach Leaf Ice Cream, Hazelnut Biscotti and a small glass of Vin Santo to either drink separately or pour over the ice cream as you would an affogato.

ASPARAGUS

BOB PERUCH

Bob Peruch is a man of principle and agrarian values. Born to hard-working Italian migrants, Bob's childhood was an education in how to grow, preserve and appreciate quality fresh food and wine, together with the value of hard physical work, good soil, quality water and clean air.

His father settled in the region in 1927, purchasing the family farm in the Middlesex Smithbrook area ten years later. The farm had sadly been abandoned as a result of the hardships incurred through the Depression years. Clearing the land and initially growing tobacco, the Peruch family farmed potatoes, cauliflower, beef cattle, dairy and a hectare of vines, the fruit from which was sold or exchanged with other migrants for customary home wine making.

Upholding the Venetian traditions of his Northern Italian parents, Bob continues to work his land, producing his own cheese, salami, honey, meat, fruit, vegetables and his sought after pinot noir that is labelled under his Christian name, Batista.

Along with working his own property, which is located 3 km away from the original family farm, Bob has spent years helping to establish some 20 different vineyards in the region, along with yearly trellising work for good friend Harvey Giblett of Newton Orchards in Manjimup.

Generous with his knowledge of the land and passionate points of view, Bob takes great pleasure in offering visitors a taste of the season, be it his latest vintage or what's been freshly harvested that day from his garden. In exchange for this kindness, Bob's wish is to instil and encourage respect for the knowledge, care and dedication required by small growers to produce quality fresh food and wine – values he sees lost in a world of big corporatised agriculture and viticulture.

Living with the seasons, Bob sees his asparagus push through the chocolate-coloured loam close to his dam each year as the bell-ringer of spring – a once yearly treat that he loves to share with friends in generous amounts, choosing not to sell commercially.

Bob's birthright was always a life of rural pursuit enriched with the traditions and seasons so integral to the culture of his family. These he will continue to preserve and share.

IF OVERCOOKED, asparagus can have an unpleasant smell and taste so be sure to cut the potatoes into a small dice so the cooking times match and your soup also retains that beautiful fresh green colour.

ASPARAGUS SOUP WITH CRÈME FRAÎCHE, CHERVIL & HAZELNUT CRUMBS

800 g asparagus

1 leek, the white part washed & roughly chopped

30 g unsalted butter

½ cup white wine

1 medium potato, peeled & small diced

1 ½ litres vegetable stock

salt flakes & freshly cracked black pepper

¼ cup cream (optional)

½ cup roasted hazelnuts, finely chopped

½ cup toasted coarse breadcrumbs

crème fraîche, to serve

½ cup chervil or dill sprigs, to garnish

SERVES 6

Trim the very ends of the asparagus and discard. Cut the tips of 18 spears approximately 5cm in length from the top and put to one side for garnish. Cut the remaining whole and partially cut spears in halves.

In a medium-sized pot, gently fry the leek in the butter until softened. Add the white wine and simmer for a couple of minutes before adding the potato, vegetable stock and halved asparagus spears. Bring to the simmer and cook for 10 minutes until the potato is soft.

Puree with a stick blender or allow to cool a little before pureeing in a food processor. Pass through a coarse sieve, pressing with a spatula to remove any fibres. Return to the pot, season to taste and stir through the ¼ cup cream.

Blanch the asparagus tips in boiling salted water and drain well. Combine the toasted breadcrumbs and roasted hazelnuts. Serve the soup with a dollop of crème fraîche, a sprinkling of the hazelnut crumb, a few chervil sprigs and three asparagus tips each to garnish.

AVOCADOS

GEORGE, STEWART & MITCHELL IPSEN

In the 60s and 70s an avocado was considered exotic, in the 80s and 90s it was thought of as fashionable and now it commonly sits next to apples and bananas in fruit bowls around the country for many months of the year, and is valued enough to still be priced per piece rather than per kilogram.

For a primary producer, this demand is what drives supply, and with strong domestic and export market forces for avocados today, an opportunity to grow in an industry sector fraught with variables often outside its control requires astute planning and business acumen along with a love of the land.

George Ipsen together his sons Stewart and Mitchell are a generational farming family, starting with George's grandfather who cleared and settled 'Mayfield' situated 15 km east of Manjimup in 1905. Over the years the Ipsen family have farmed cattle, potatoes, cauliflower, broccoli and apples, and in 1996 George planted his first avocado orchard at Mayfield.

Today George, Stewart and Mitchell have individually invested and worked with other partners to establish joint venture projects under the Ipsen Management Trust, building vertically integrated avocado growing, packing and distribution businesses in Pemberton and Manjimup. These collectively cover 260 hectares of mostly Hass variety avocado orchards.

Not without difficulties, avocados are a unique and temperature-sensitive fruit to grow, with flowering and fruit set in October and November then harvested from November to March the following year. This means the trees carry two crops at the same time, requiring up to 150 litres of high-quality water per tree per day through the summer months. 'The long tree-hanging time contributes to the superior flavour and oil content of our fruit, which together with our dry summer environment that prevents internal black rot enables us to grow a quality product our customers can have confidence in,' George explains.

'When I entered the industry 16 years ago, consumption was around 1 ½ kilos per person per year. It is now 12 to 13 kilos in mature international markets. Avocado production is undergoing rapid growth in our region, with total West Australian avocado production expected to reach 4 million trays in 2014 to 2015. We have a big job ahead to grow the markets (through value adding) and meet consumer and grower expectations.'

Arguably, there is no better example of a primary product than an avocado in a fruit bowl to indicate recent food trends in Australia. It's the only fruit that contains healthy mono-unsaturated fat and has a delicious buttery rich taste and creamy texture suited to so many different flavour combinations. A pleasure not lost on our Southern Forests growers working hard to keep them in our fruit bowls into the future.

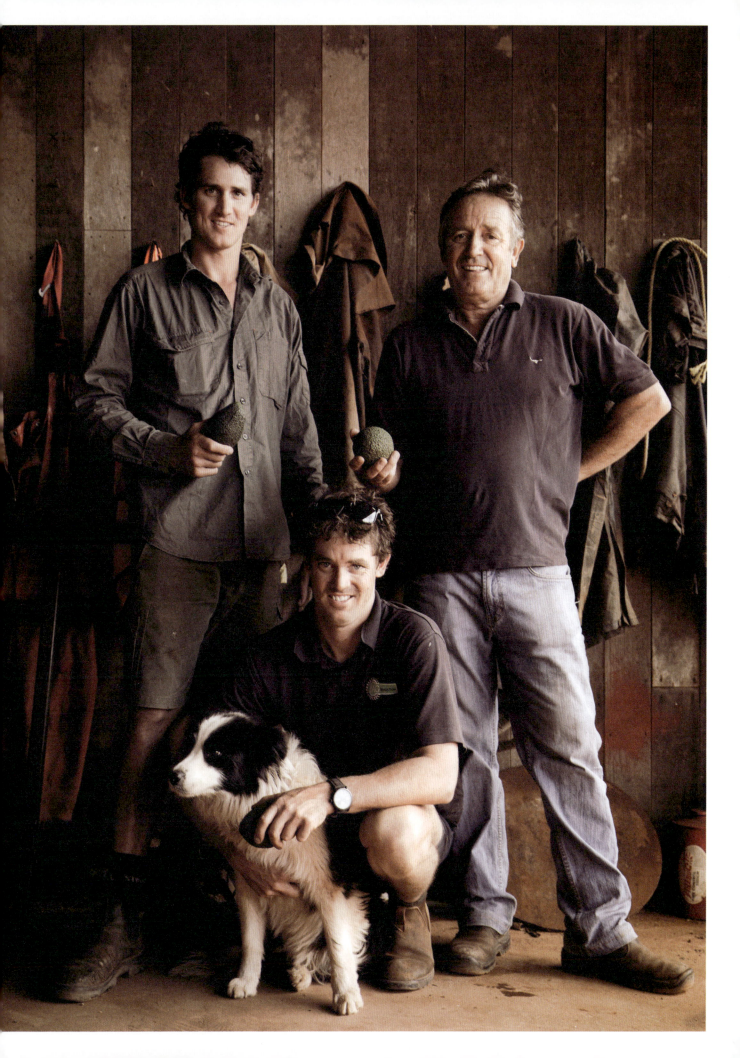

THE INSPIRATION for this retro-style entrée was a prawn cocktail that was served in the cavity of an avocado half. Interestingly, cinnamon and avocados are from the same botanical family, Lauraceae, and have a wonderful flavour affinity.

AVOCADO WITH LIME, PICKLED GINGER, CINNAMON, TOASTED PINE NUTS & PURPLE BASIL

2 ripe Hass avocados

1 tbsp Japanese-style pickled ginger, finely sliced

¼ cup toasted pine nuts

1 lime, rind & pith removed & finely diced

2 tbsp (+ extra) extra virgin olive oil or avocado oil

¼ tsp (+ extra) ground cinnamon

salt flakes & freshly cracked black pepper

½ cup purple basil leaves

SERVES 4, ENTRÉE SIZE

Halve the avocados, remove the seeds and, using a large spoon, scoop the flesh out of the skin in one motion so the avocado half is intact. Cut a sliver of avocado from the curved side to make a flat surface so the avocado sits flat on the plate. Finely dice the avocado slivers and place in the cavity where the seed was. Combine the pickled ginger, pine nuts, lime, extra virgin olive oil and ground cinnamon with a little seasoning and divide evenly amongst the four avocado halves. Garnish with the purple basil leaves, drizzle over a little more oil and sprinkle a pinch of ground cinnamon on each filled avocado before serving.

NASTURTIUM LEAVES add a delicious peppery taste to any salad but be sure to use young leaves as the older leaves can be coarse and chewy. Substitute with rocket or watercress if need be.

AVOCADO, ORANGE, FENNEL, RADISH, NASTURTIUM & WILD OLIVE SALAD

1 orange
1 tbsp lemon or lime juice
100 ml avocado oil or
extra virgin olive oil
salt flakes & freshly
cracked black pepper
2 ripe Hass avocados
1 lrg handful sml nasturtium leaves
1 fennel bulb, thinly sliced
4 radishes, thinly sliced
½ cup sml wild olives or halved
pitted Kalamata olives

**SERVES 4 AS AN
ACCOMPANYING SALAD**

Cut away the rind and pith of the orange. Collecting the juice in a bowl, as you hold the peeled orange, cut out the segments between the membranes. Squeeze out the juice from the remaining membranes into the bowl. Combine orange juice with the lemon juice and whisk in the avocado oil, seasoning to taste.

Halve the avocados, remove the seed and scoop out of the skin with a large spoon. Thinly slice. Layer the avocado slices and nasturtium leaves with the fennel, radish and orange segments. Scatter over the wild olives before drizzling with the dressing and seasoning with some salt flakes and freshly cracked black pepper.

BABY SPINACH & ICEBERG LETTUCE

DAVID EAST

Iceberg lettuce has taken a fair old snubbing from the fancier gourmet types in the last 25 years; however, it is still the main lettuce variety grown in Australia and, arguably, the most versatile.

It has been cooked and served with an oil and vinegar dressing by the Romans, made into a soup by the French, served as a wrap called Sang Choi Bao by the Chinese and, of course, included in millions of American-style burgers at fast food outlets around the world.

David East together with his wife Lee and family have been commercially growing iceberg lettuce since 1999, and baby spinach more recently, for the demanding 'QSR' (quick service restaurants) market and pre-packaged supermarket industry. They farm a 300-acre property in the Dingup area east of Manjimup.

David's grandfather migrated as a young boy from England to Northcliffe in the 1920s, working as a sleeper cutter and labouring on various farms until establishing a bulldozing business with his son, clearing large areas of land in the region and building dams. David's father Mervyn then went out on his own in the 1970s, growing cattle and then blue gums in Northcliffe before purchasing the property in Dingup in 1977.

Throughout the 1980s they ran 5,000 crossbred sheep for the wool and meat market, 300 descendants from which still remain as part of David's rotation cycle. Transitioning from beef and sheep to horticulture – focusing at the time on cauliflower for the export market – presented many challenges, but valuable advice from local growers assisted them greatly during this establishing period.

Lettuce is one of the most difficult crops to produce for the highly cosmetic-focused market. 'Many people think lesser grades go into the food service industry, but that's not the case. The processors are just as fussy as the supermarkets for perfect, blemish free product,' David explains.

David and Lee's growing season for iceberg starts at the beginning of December and continues through to the middle of May. Baby spinach grows from the beginning of November to the end of May; the harvesting of it has been aided by a purpose-built machine that David designed.

Innovation has been the key to their ongoing success, and most recently the introduction of natural bio-fumigants in the form of mustard used as a green manure has resulted in a significant reduction in disease and pests.

'Mustard plants are cultivated and then rolled and mulched into the soil no more than 20 minutes after the plant is cut, sealing the mustard gases into the soil which in effect cleans it of potential problems and also provides organic matter,' David explains.

Establishing their own seed nursery has given them control over the growing cycle. It takes 6 to 8 weeks from sowing the seed to planting out the seedling and then another 6 to 8 weeks until harvest. The lettuces are then cut in the morning; vacuum cooled dropping the temperature to 2 ˚C in 20 minutes; and then delivered into Perth the same day, ensuring quality and optimum shelf life.

Humble iceberg lettuce and the more fashionable baby spinach are staples in a long list of produce grown in this abundant region. This produce reaches all corners of Western Australia and is probably on our plates every day – whether it's fancy or not you can be sure it's of the highest quality possible.

LOVAGE IS a perennial herb that looks a little like young celery leaves and has a similar savoury taste that seasons any dish it's added to with delicious results.

ICEBERG WEDGES WITH SALAD CREAM, LOVAGE & SUNFLOWER SEEDS

1 whole iceberg lettuce
2 tbsp apple cider vinegar
1 tsp caster sugar
½ tsp Dijon mustard
½ tsp salt
1 cup fresh pouring cream
4 tsp sunflower seeds
½ cup lovage leaves, torn
freshly cracked black pepper

SERVES 4

Remove the large outer leaves and cut the inner iceberg lettuce into eight wedges. Lightly rinse and drain well. Whisk the vinegar, sugar, mustard and salt together to combine before incorporating the cream. Place the iceberg wedges on a platter and evenly pour over the cream. Scatter over the sunflower seeds and lovage and serve with freshly cracked black pepper.

ALTHOUGH ICEBERG is generally considered only a salad green, cooked lettuce has been used in French and Chinese cooking for many years. As it is 95% water, the key when applying heat is to make it hot and fast. Sumac is a dried berry that is finely ground, brick-red in colour and has a delicious lemony tang.

WILTED ICEBERG & BABY SPINACH WITH LEMON, GARLIC, CUMIN SEED & SUMAC

1 iceberg lettuce
olive oil
4 garlic cloves, thinly sliced
1 tsp cumin seeds, roughly crushed in a mortar & pestle
2 handfuls baby spinach
4 lemon wedges
½ tsp sumac
salt flakes & freshly cracked black pepper

SERVES 4, AS A SIDE DISH

Remove the large outer leaves and cut the inner iceberg lettuce into eight wedges. Lightly rinse if needed and drain well. Allow to dry as much as possible.

Heat a little olive oil in a large heavy-based frying pan. Gently fry a quarter of the garlic and cumin seeds until the garlic begins to change colour. Place two iceberg wedges into the pan cut-side facing downwards and fry for 20 seconds before turning to fry the other cut side of the wedge. Take care as if there is still water on the lettuce the pan will spit. Repeat another three times, cooking two wedges of lettuce at a time.

Place the baby spinach in the bottom of individual bowls or on a platter and serve the wilted iceberg wedges on top, scattering over the cooked garlic slices and cumin. Serve with lemon wedges and garnish with sumac, salt flakes and freshly cracked black pepper.

BAMBOO SHOOTS & BETEL LEAVES

KEVIN FITZPATRICK & 'JEEP' PUNTIP BINSIRAWANIT

Kevin Fitzpatrick and Jeep Binsirawanit's property 'Bamboo Springs' is located deep in the karri forest approximately 20 km south-west of Pemberton. Originally from New Zealand, Kevin settled there 40 years ago, meeting Jeep in Thailand some years later. Jeep subsequently moved to Australia to live with Kevin in 1999, bringing her culinary and gardening skills with her.

Growing 150 varieties of bamboo for construction and culinary purposes, Kevin's background in steel erecting and Jeep's knowledge of bamboo shoots for various Thai dishes make them unique producers in the Southern Forests who contribute valuable culinary diversity to this productive region.

Along with bamboo, their extensive garden also produces betel leaves, various Asian herbs, fresh chillies and other vegetables and fruit that they sell in their roadside stall located on Old Vasse Road. Aside from their roadside stall and local restaurants, Jeep and Kevin also supply directly to Thai restaurants in Perth.

Bamboo shoots are available in March and April and are best when young and just harvested, as due to hydrocyanic acid reacting with the sugars and starches they soon turn bitter. Preserving or cooking the bamboo shoots when fresh retains their crisp, nutty taste that adds valuable crunch and depth to many different dishes.

Betel leaves are from a perennial vine that requires long pole-based construction for support and are the basis of the traditional Thai snack miang. They are used as a wrapper and filled with various crunchy and fresh ingredients such as roasted coconut and peanuts, chopped lime, shallots, ginger, bird's eye chilli and a dressing made with palm sugar. They're available from December through to April.

THESE PRESERVED bamboo shoots are nothing like the tinned version available in supermarkets. With a firmer texture and delicious sweet, root-vegetable-like taste, Jeep uses them year round in stir-fries, curries and soups.

JEEP'S PRESERVED BAMBOO SHOOTS

1 kg fresh young bamboo shoots, peeled
1 tbsp rice flour
1 ½ tbsp salt

Slice the bamboo shoots across the grain into 2 mm thick slices and wash well under cold running water. Drain and transfer to a large bowl.

Combine the rice flour and salt and gently massage and toss through the bamboo shoots for 5 to 10 minutes until the shoots have softened a little and given off a good amount of liquid.

Pack the bamboo slices into a sealable jar, pour over the extracted liquid and store for a minimum of one month and up to twelve months.

Prior to using in stir-fries or curries, rinse the preserved bamboo shoots in cold water, place in a pot, cover with cold water and bring to the boil with a little salt. Simmer until just softened but still with a little crunch.

A DISH in Chui Lee Luk's wonderful cookbook 'Green Pickled Peaches' inspired this recipe. I've built upon it to create a rich, crunchy and salty taste and a textural contrast that's a joy with a glass of bubbles. Substitute the caraway flowers and seeds with fennel pollen that can be purchased online through spice merchants.

SPICED BETEL LEAF FRITTER, MARRON, AIR-DRIED BEEF, SALMON ROE & CARAWAY FLOWERS

75 g yellow split peas
¼ tsp dried chilli flakes
1 sml shallot, finely chopped
½ tsp fresh ginger, grated
2 tsp curry leaves, finely chopped
½ tsp salt
2 free-range egg whites
12 betel leaves
1 lrg live marron
rice bran or sunflower oil, for frying
50 g air-dried beef, thinly sliced
2 tsp salmon roe
caraway flowers & fresh seeds,
to garnish

SERVES 4

Soak the yellow split peas overnight. Drain well before placing in a blender together with the dried chilli flakes, shallot, fresh ginger, curry leaves, salt and one of the egg whites to make a loose paste.

Brush the back of each betel leaf with the other egg white before spreading 1 teaspoon of the paste over the brushed egg white. Leave to dry uncovered in the refrigerator for an hour.

Place the marron in the freezer for 20 to 30 minutes until the marron no longer moves but is not yet frozen, before cooking in a pot of boiling salted water for 2 minutes. Plunge immediately into a sink of ice-cold water. Remove from the shell, discard the alimentary canal, rinse and thinly slice.

Heat the rice bran oil in a deep pot to a depth of 3 cm until 170 °C. Deep fry the betel leaves until golden. Drain on absorbent paper.

Top with slices of air-dried beef and marron. Serve immediately garnished with salmon roe and caraway flowers and fresh seeds.

BEEF

JOHN DELLA GOLA

Food security is a term that was only recently formalised at the World Food Conference held in Rome in 1974, and yet it's a concept that various cultures around the world have known for centuries.

Italians, along with other southern and eastern European cultures that migrated to Australia after the Second World War, knew the threat of an insecure food supply and as a consequence were extremely resourceful, valuing every part of the plant or animal they could grow and conserve.

John Della Gola's parents, Quirino and Giuseppina Della Gola, separately migrated from the Valtellina and Verona regions in Northern Italy in the late 1940s, meeting in Kalgoorlie and settling on 100 acres situated 10 km south-west of Pemberton in a small area called Flybrook. Here they hand dug and cleared land, living and farming subsistently with dairy cows, growing potatoes and operating a local telephone exchange. They moved closer to Pemberton in the late 1960s, and it was here that John spent the majority of his childhood.

Purchasing another farm closer to Northcliffe in the late 1970s, John and his wife Helen raised five children and continued with potato and milk production. Due to the deregulation of the dairy industry in 2000, John decided instead to raise beef cattle to supply the local market.

Today, John and his sons Matthew and Joseph raise up to 6,000 head of predominately Angus, Murray Grey and Shorthorn cattle for high-quality yearling beef. The cattle is grown on their Northcliffe property, the original family farm in Pemberton and a property east of Manjimup at Tonebridge. The majority of their cattle are sold through the Dardanup Butchering Company, supplying 20,000 kg of meat into the local market each week.

Despite farming in a high rainfall region with abundant pasture for five months of the year (supplemented with their own silage and assisted with grain the other seven months of the year), the yearly rises in cost of production without the equivalent increases in return have presented enormous challenges in recent times. 'We love what we do, but receiving 1975 prices and having to pay 2014 bills makes it unsustainable,' John explains.

The process and high cost of growing and distribution has become a complex network of obstacles. John sees this only changing with the consumer valuing quality beef enough to pay more for it, as well as choosing secondary cuts of meat, thus creating demand for the whole animal resulting in less waste. He also believes government support is necessary for greater competition amongst local export-ready abattoirs. 'Thirty years ago we had twenty-six export abattoirs in WA. We now have three,' says John.

Mitigating threats to local food supply and therefore security in years to come is of great concern to growers like John. 'It's vital that the public are made aware that supporting and valuing local beef enough to pay more for it ensures quality and supply from local growers who at the moment only barely manage to operate.'

Registering his own brand 'Della Gola Prime', John will continue to innovate and combine resourceful production methods to produce quality local beef. In turn, this will be a family business viable enough for his son Matthew to continue on with, passing on the legacy and cultural values inherent to their family's history and success.

KOHLRABI IS a vegetable from the brassica family. Its juicy swollen stem looks a little like a turnip but it tastes like sweet cabbage and adds a lovely crunch to contrast with the soft sugar-cured beef. If unavailable use thinly sliced daikon radish instead.

SUGAR-CURED BEEF WITH KOHLRABI, FENNEL, APPLE, CAPERS & SHEEPS' CHEESE

2 cups (+ 2 tsp) raw caster sugar

2 cups salt

3 tbsp fennel seeds,
dry roasted & coarsely crushed

3 tbsp coriander seeds,
dry roasted & coarsely crushed

1 tbsp black peppercorns,
coarsely crushed

1 ½ cups Pernod

1 sml beef fillet
(approx. 1 kg), trimmed

1 tbsp Dijon mustard

100 ml olive oil

2 tbsp lemon juice

salt flakes & freshly
cracked black pepper

1 sml kohlrabi, peeled & thinly sliced

1 Granny Smith apple, peeled, cored
& julienned

½ fennel bulb, thinly sliced

1 cup hard sheeps' cheese, shaved

1 tbsp baby capers, rinsed

¼ cup fresh dill sprigs

SERVES 8

Mix together the 2 cups raw caster sugar, 2 cups salt, fennel and coriander seeds, 1 tbsp coarsely crushed black pepper and Pernod. Place a piece of wide (or two overlapping pieces) plastic wrap in the base of a deep tray. Spread half the salt mixture on the plastic wrap before laying the beef fillet on top. Coat the fillet in the remaining salt mixture. Lift the edges of the plastic wrap over the top of the fillet and roll tightly to completely wrap the fillet. Place a small board on top of the fillet before weighing down with a heavy mortar and pestle and full cans. Leave to cure in the refrigerator for a minimum of 24 hours or maximum of 3 days. Remove the fillet from the cure and rinse clean, rolling in a tea towel to completely dry before thinly slicing with a sharp knife.

Make the dressing by whisking together the remaining 2 tsp raw caster sugar, Dijon mustard, olive oil, lemon juice and seasoning. Adjust with a little cold water until the consistency of pouring cream.

Layer 100 g per person of the sliced cured beef together with the kohlrabi, apple, fennel and sheeps' cheese. Drizzle over the mustard dressing and garnish with the capers and fresh dill sprigs. Serve with extra freshly cracked black pepper.

ADD A little more stock to this melt-in-the-mouth tender beef and serve as a wonderful braise with creamy mashed potatoes or to fold through wide pasta ribbons. For the best quality pickled walnuts choose the local West Australian produced Pretsel Vineyard Pickled Walnuts from Manjimup over the imported versions.

BEEF CHEEK, FIELD MUSHROOM & PICKLED WALNUT PIE

4 lrg beef cheeks, trimmed

salt flakes & freshly
cracked black pepper

3 tbsp olive oil

1 onion, roughly chopped

3 cloves garlic, roughly chopped

1 carrot, roughly chopped

2 sticks celery, roughly chopped

3 bay leaves

8 sprigs fresh thyme

1 x 375 ml bottle Coopers Extra Stout

500 ml beef stock

½ kg field mushrooms, halved &
thickly sliced

260 g leeks, roughly chopped

30 g unsalted butter

¼ cup flour

3 tbsp crème fraîche or sour cream

160 g pickled walnuts, thickly sliced

1 tbsp fresh thyme, finely chopped

3 sheets Carême puff pastry

1 free-range egg

3 tbsp milk

MAKES 10 LRG MUFFIN-SIZED PIES

Preheat oven to 150 °C. Season the beef cheeks well, before browning in the olive oil in a deep, heavy-based, ovenproof lidded pot. Reserve beef to the side. Gently sauté the onion, garlic, carrot and celery in the same pot until just softened. Add the bay leaves, fresh thyme and browned beef cheeks. Pour in the stout, stock and enough water if needed to just cover. Place a piece of baking paper directly onto the surface, cover with the lid, bring to a gentle simmer and transfer to the oven. Cook for 3 hours or until the cheeks begin to fall apart. Strain 500 ml of the cooking juices from the beef cheeks and reserve. Loosely cover the cooked beef cheeks with aluminium foil and allow to cool.

Sauté the mushrooms and leeks in the butter until all the juices have evaporated. Season, and sprinkle over the flour while stirring. Gently continue to cook and stir for 2 minutes. Gradually pour in the reserved 500 ml cooking juices while stirring. Simmer gently for 5 minutes, stirring periodically, until the sauce has thickened. Stir through the crème fraîche and cook another 2 minutes. Reserve to the side.

Gently pull the beef cheeks apart into small bite-sized pieces. Fold through the mushroom sauce together with the pickled walnuts and chopped fresh thyme. Cover with a piece of baking paper directly on the surface and leave to cool before refrigerating. RECIPE CONTINUES >

Using a large circle biscuit cutter, cut 10 pie lids the diameter of the top of a large muffin in a muffin baking tray, from the sheets of puff pastry. Gather the pastry scraps and roll out until slightly thinner than the lids, and line 10 large muffin cups in a multi-cup non-stick muffin baking tin, leaving a 1 cm overhang of pastry on each.

Beat the egg and milk together to make an egg wash, and brush the pastry edges of the pie base and one side of the pie lids. Fill with the chilled pie filling, then place the lids on top, egg wash side down. Using the tines of a fork, press around the edges of each pie to adhere the lids with the bases. Trim away the excess pastry by using the same biscuit cutter as for the tops.

Egg wash the tops of the pies and gently cut a concentric pattern on each pie using the tip of a paring knife. Refrigerate for 10 minutes before baking in a preheated 220 °C oven for 10 minutes. Reduce the temperature to 180 °C and continue to bake for 20 to 30 minutes.

Allow to sit for 10 minutes before gently removing from the tins and serving.

RIB EYE beef is a premium cut for celebrations, which when cooked as a whole roast makes for spectacular presentation. The smoked tomatoes and kale pesto are equally wonderful accompaniments to a grilled rump steak, or slow-cooked and thinly sliced pickled silverside.

ROAST RIB EYE BEEF WITH SMOKED TOMATOES & KALE PESTO

Roast Rib Eye

3.4 – 3.6 kg rib eye beef
olive oil
sea salt flakes &
cracked black pepper
8 x 12 – 15 cm long rosemary sprigs

Kale Pesto

300 g kale, ribs removed &
coarsely chopped
½ cup pine nuts, lightly toasted
½ cup extra virgin olive oil
juice & zest of a small lemon
2 cloves garlic
½ tsp (+ extra) salt
freshly cracked black pepper
1 cup parmesan cheese, finely grated

Smoked Tomatoes

2 cups tea leaves
2 cups rice
2 cups soft brown sugar
1 kg heirloom tomatoes of varying
shapes & colours

SERVES 4

Rub the beef with a little olive oil and season generously. Tie the rosemary sprigs onto the beef with cotton string or butcher's twine. Allow the beef to come to room temperature. Preheat oven to 220 °C. Place the rib eye on a rack in a baking tray and roast for 20 minutes. Reduce the heat to 180 °C and cook for 1 ½ hours for medium rare. Cover loosely with aluminium foil and leave to rest for 45 minutes.

To make the kale pesto, blanch the kale in boiling salted water, cooling under cold running water. Drain well before rolling in a tea towel to dry. Place in a food processor with the pine nuts, extra virgin olive oil, lemon, garlic and seasoning. Process until a coarse puree. Transfer to a bowl and fold through the grated parmesan. Check seasoning and adjust if needed.

To prepare the smoked tomatoes, preheat a hooded barbecue. Line a deep, lidded baking tray with four layers of aluminium foil. Combine the tea leaves, rice and soft brown sugar and spoon into the tray in an even layer. Place a wire rack into the tray that sits above the rice mixture. Lightly rub each tomato with a little olive oil and place on the rack. Put the lid on the tray and place directly on the barbecue grill. Put the barbecue hood down to cover. Smoke for 20 to 30 minutes until the tomatoes have partially collapsed and are slightly burnished.

Reheat the roast beef in a 200 °C oven for 10 minutes before carving and serving with the kale pesto and smoked tomatoes on the side.

BEETROOT & KALE

WAYNE EDWARDS

Contrary to the stereotype, organic farmer Wayne Edwards saw the rationale of farming without chemicals as a logical business decision rather than philosophical choice, making a decision 15 years ago to change the way his family had always farmed. 'A healthy soil grows healthy premium foods that yield a higher return and supports healthier bodies,' explains Wayne.

Through being on a local committee formed to tackle soil erosion, Wayne saw that soils with greater microbial activity and organic matter acted like sponges for water, which in turn were able to support healthier plants and therefore yield better quality produce that could return a higher price.

Wayne's father, Doug, had, like his father and Scottish grandfather before him, previously farmed conventionally – growing potatoes, raising cattle and, during the buoyant late 1970s and 1980s, producing cauliflowers for the successful export market. 'The soils changed (though) and we had to make decisions to do things differently. So we were happy to let Wayne take the organic path.' Doug recalls.

'Bioveg' is the brand under which Wayne now sells his organic kale, beetroot, potatoes, broccoli and cauliflower. In addition to the vegetables that are grown on the family farm, Wayne and his wife Anita also grow Demeter-certified biodynamic avocados and a small amount of plums on their home property, 'Tree of Love Resort', west of Manjimup.

Produce from both farms are sold into the Perth and interstate markets. They also sell at the Manjimup Farmers Market where Wayne's parents, Doug and Kay, have sold the family's produce since its early beginnings.

'The Southern Forests area has the best West Australian soils, high mineral loam over a clay base. But chemical farming is acid farming which burns the soil,' Wayne explains. 'Organic farming is alkaline farming and our bodies need live, alkaline food to prevent sickness and disease.'

Despite the success of converting to organic farming, incorporating modern GPS farm technologies and irrigation, and their shared packing shed in Manjimup, Doug sees his future in farming changing. 'Each year our input costs keep rising but our returns are not. Smaller growers cannot afford to keep going, so we are forced to become bigger and bigger.'

As Wayne's children are reluctant to take over the work and responsibilities of primary production, his desire to explore the world beyond the vegie patch together with supporting Anita's raw food business calls for another leap. For now, however, the Edwards family will continue farming organically with the pioneering spirit of their Scottish forebears over 100 years ago.

THE SUCCESS of this salad combination is in the sum of its many parts. Purslane is Portulaca oleracea: a common garden weed that's traditionally included in the Lebanese tomato and bread salad fattoush and also included in this salad for its thick, juicy leaves and salty taste. Substitute with baby spinach if difficult to find.

ROAST BEETROOT, POMEGRANATE MOLASSES, PRESERVED ORANGE, LABNA, TRUFFLE OIL, PURSLANE & ROASTED HAZELNUT SALAD

Preserved Oranges

lrg sterilised clip-top glass preserving jars
fresh in-season oranges, washed
coarse salt
whole cloves
cassia sticks
fresh bay leaves

Labna

500 ml thick Greek yoghurt
½ tsp salt

Roast Beetroot, Pomegranate Molasses, Truffle Oil, Purslane & Roasted Hazelnut Salad

400 g raw beetroot, peeled
4 tsp pomegranate molasses
2 tbsp olive oil
3 tsp red wine vinegar
sea salt flakes & freshly cracked black pepper
1 preserved orange or lemon quarter
1 handful purslane leaves, washed
1 cup labna
¾ cup roasted hazelnuts, roughly chopped
black truffle oil

SERVES 4

PRESERVED ORANGES

Cut a cross into the orange, three-quarters of the way through from the stem end downwards. Sprinkle a little salt and two or three whole cloves into each orange. Push the quarters of the fruit back together and then tightly pack into the glass jars with two cassia sticks and three fresh bay leaves per glass jar. Squeeze some extra orange juice to fill the jar and clip the lid on. Refill with extra juice every 2 days for the first week if needed. Store in a cool place for a minimum of a month prior to use.

LABNA

Stir the salt into the yoghurt before scraping into a dampened muslin–lined sieve. Gather and tie the loose end of the muslin together and hang to drain 6 hours or overnight.

SALAD

Preheat oven to 180 °C. Thinly slice the beetroot using a mandolin and evenly place the slices on a baking tray. Drizzle over the pomegranate molasses, olive oil and vinegar. Season with salt and freshly cracked black pepper before covering with aluminium foil and baking in the oven for 20 to 25 minutes until the beetroot is tender. Leave to cool. Season to taste and adjust with extra red wine vinegar if more acidity needed.

Remove the flesh of the preserved orange, rinse under cold water and slice the rind thinly. Divide the cooked beetroot slices with the cooking juices and purslane between four plates. Place small dollops of labna on top and then scatter over the roasted hazelnuts and preserved orange slices. Drizzle with a little truffle oil and serve with freshly cracked black pepper.

ZA'ATAR IS a Middle Eastern seasoning mix of dried thyme, sesame, sumac and salt that's combined in this recipe with ground roasted wattleseed to accompany and season bite-sized wraps in much the same way as dukkah is served as a dry dip with olive oil and flatbread.

PICKLED KALE & FRESH RICOTTA WRAPS WITH WATTLESEED ZA'ATAR

¼ cup salt

500 ml apple cider vinegar

500 ml water

250 g raw caster sugar

2 tbsp caraway seeds

2 fresh bay leaves

8 large kale leaves, rib & stem removed

500 g fresh ricotta, drained

2 tbsp za'atar

1 tsp ground roasted wattleseed

SERVES 4 AS A STARTER

Bring the salt, vinegar, water, sugar, caraway seeds and bay leaves to the boil, stirring to dissolve the sugar and salt. Lay the kale leaves in a deep ceramic, glass or stainless steel bowl or container and pour over the hot pickling syrup. Leave to cool and then place in the refrigerator overnight.

Remove and drain the kale well. Cut each kale leaf in half and roll a teaspoon of fresh ricotta up in the kale leaf. Mix the ground wattleseed together with the za'atar and place a tablespoon on each plate to serve with four wraps per person.

THIS IS a delicious version of the classic Caesar Salad that makes a sturdy lunch during winter. Transport the components separately to easily combine together at a picnic when 'cabin-fever' sets in during the colder months and the beauty of a winter landscape calls.

CRISPY KALE CAESAR-STYLE SALAD

2 lrg bunches or 4 whole curly kale

4 thick slices sourdough bread, roughly torn into chunks

olive oil

¼ cup crème fraîche

1 tsp Dijon mustard

4 anchovy fillets, finely chopped

1 tbsp lemon juice

salt flakes & freshly cracked black pepper

250 g Blackwood Valley organic beef pastrami, thinly sliced

4 free-range eggs, hard-boiled, peeled & halved

1 cup parmesan cheese, thinly shaved

freshly cracked black pepper

SERVES 4

Preheat oven to 220 °C. Cut away the rib and stem end of the kale leaves and reserve for a soup or vegetable dish. Spread the leaves and sourdough chunks on separate baking trays, and lightly drizzle both with olive oil. Roast in the oven for 20 to 30 minutes, turning them over after 10 minutes and roasting until golden and crispy.

Whisk together the crème fraîche, Dijon mustard, anchovies and lemon juice with a little seasoning adjusting with cold water until the consistency of pouring cream.

Lay the roasted kale and crispy sourdough croutons on a platter and nestle the pastrami and boiled egg halves evenly in and around the kale. Scatter over the parmesan and then drizzle over the dressing. Serve with extra freshly cracked black pepper.

BISCUITS, CHEESE & WHITE BEANS

MARY BORSHOFF

Throughout history, food has played a vital and defining role in the development of culture and community. When relocating, new migrants bring their food traditions with them and, for many, traditions of growing, preparing and sharing food are as important and as comforting as the few belongings they bring with them.

Macedonians arrived in Manjimup and Bridgetown during the inter-war period and early 1940s. Mary Borshoff (nee Tassos) was born in the early 1950s to parents who had settled in Bridgetown; her father worked in a flax mill in Boyup Brook making rope. As for other Macedonian migrants, strong family ties and their own local community were critically important for survival and happiness in their new home.

Children born of these migrants were raised within this tight-knit community, but also had to adapt and assimilate as young Australians. 'I loved the free Australian way of thinking,' Mary recalls, 'but when we returned home from school and walked through the door, we were Macedonian. We had a kind of double life of which I loved both sides.'

Mary met George, also of Macedonian heritage, through the local social networks, which at the time included dances held in local halls. They married and lived with George's parents on the family farm in West Manjimup for the first three years, during which Mary watched and honed her growing and food preparation skills with George's mother. 'She was a wonderfully instinctive cook, preparing traditional foods as easily as breathing air,' remembers Mary.

Macedonian food is predominately based around a subsistence farming culture in which vegetables, dried beans, peppers, tomatoes, cheese and bread are the predominate base. 'Due to poverty, meat was scarce and enjoyed only for celebratory meals, so dried beans and home-made feta-style cheese were our main sources of protein, which we now know are healthy,' Mary explains.

Desserts and sweet foods were influenced by the Greek and Turkish traditions of syrupy cakes, pastries and biscuits including the ubiquitous crescent-shaped almond shortbreads heavily dusted with icing sugar.

Non-hybrid seed was saved from year to year, and, when planted, extra amounts were included in case neighbours, friends or family had suffered a loss of their own supply. Fresh produce was also traditionally offered as gifts throughout the year. 'Being resourceful, looking after each other, saving and not wasting anything allowed us to survive and prosper,' says Mary.

Despite the technology-driven global culture her grandchildren are now growing up in, Mary offers a taste of their family heritage through the traditional dishes she still prepares, and by teaching them a little of the Macedonian language. This cultural legacy has shaped not only their own family history, but was also the foundation from which the early settlers developed the region into what it is today.

I HAVE reduced the quantities of Mary's original recipe for her wonderful sesame biscuits; however, after you've tried them I'm sure you'll consider doubling this recipe next time!

MARY'S MACEDONIAN SESAME SEED BISCUITS & KOURABIEDES

Sesame Seed Biscuits

¼ cup white wine
¼ cup caster sugar
125 ml sunflower or grapeseed oil
½ tsp vanilla extract
1 ¾ cups self-raising flour
¼ cup sesame seeds

MAKES APPROX. 40

Kourabiedes

180 g unsalted
butter, softened
185 g (+ extra) icing sugar
1 tsp vanilla extract
1 free-range egg yolk
250 g plain flour
90 g almond meal
½ tsp baking powder
pinch of salt

MAKES APPROX. 20

SESAME SEED BISCUITS

Preheat oven to 180 °C and line baking trays with baking paper. Combine the wine, sugar, oil and vanilla extract. Place the self-raising flour in a large bowl, make a well, pour in the wine mixture and mix together to make a stiff dough. Shape into walnut-size balls, roll in sesame seeds, lightly press the tops with a fork and place on the baking trays allowing 1 cm space between each biscuit. Bake 20 to 25 minutes until a light golden colour. Cool on a wire rack. Store in an airtight container.

KOURABIEDES

Preheat oven to 180 °C and line baking trays with baking paper. Cream the butter and sugar until light and fluffy. Add the vanilla and egg yolk and beat until well combined. Add the flour, almond meal, baking powder and salt and gently beat until smooth. Turn the mixture out on a floured work surface. Form walnut-sized amounts of dough into crescent shapes and place on the baking trays. Bake 12 to 15 minutes until a light golden colour. Cool on a wire rack before sifting over extra icing sugar to coat the biscuits. Store in an airtight container.

AS WITH many recipes handed down from one generation to another, specific quantities are not as important as the method. In this recipe for Mary's Macedonian Cheese, Mary has focused more on the variables, which as you can read are many when it comes to cheese making. Practise will result in personalising your own method which will lead to perfection.

MARY'S MACEDONIAN CHEESE

Milk your cow and strain the milk through fine muslin or a sieve, then add about a teaspoon of rennet to 10 to 15 litres of blood-temperature milk. By the time you have walked home from the dairy it will be perfectly mixed.

Test the temperature of the milk with your finger. If the milk is too cold it will take a long time to set a curd, and it will always remain a soft weak cheese. On the other hand if the milk is too hot it becomes stringy. Wait for milk to set; this takes about half an hour. Keep milk at this mild room temperature until strained.

Cut the curd into cubes right to the bottom of container (the size of the cubes makes a difference to the finished cheese). Wait about half an hour, strain into a muslin cloth and then tie a knot and hang in the shade of a tree for a pear-shaped lump of cheese. Alternatively, fashion into the desired shape over a flat strainer in your cheese room.

In another half hour cut into squares, sprinkle cooking salt over all sides and place into a container. The cheese will now release more whey, but you'll still need to add more saved whey to completely cover the cheese.

Problems can arise at every stage of the cheese making. The temperature of the day, the season, the condition of rennet, whether the cow has her calf by her side (she can separate her milk to save the cream for the calf and you end up with skim milk), whether the grass is green or dry, can all make a difference to the finished cheese.

THIS CREAMY white bean puree makes a delicious start to a meal and can be served as an alternative to hummus. It's also great in sandwiches or even served alongside meat dishes instead of mashed potato.

MANJIMUP WHITE BEAN PUREE WITH BUCKWHEAT LAVOSH

Manjimup White Bean Puree
(Makes 3 cups)

250 g Manjimup white beans or dried cannellini beans

3 cloves garlic

1 fresh bay leaf

sea salt

1 tbsp fresh rosemary, finely chopped

⅓ cup extra virgin olive oil
(plus extra, for serving)

freshly cracked black pepper

Buckwheat Lavosh

300 g plain strong flour

50 g buckwheat flour

1 tsp caster sugar

1 tsp salt

150 ml water

2 free-range egg whites

30 g butter, melted

semolina, for rolling

SERVES 6

MANJIMUP WHITE BEAN PUREE

Soak the white beans overnight or for several hours. Drain before putting into a large saucepan with water to cover 5 cm above the beans, together with the garlic cloves and fresh bay leaf. Bring to the boil and simmer until just tender.

Add salt to taste and cook further until the beans are soft. Drain, reserving the cooking liquid. Allow the beans to cool a little before pureeing in a food processor together with the rosemary, extra virgin olive oil, ⅓ cup of the reserved cooking liquid and freshly cracked black pepper.

Leave to cool to room temperature before serving drizzled with a little extra virgin olive oil.

BUCKWHEAT LAVOSH

Place the dry ingredients in the bowl of a food processor. With the motor running, pour in the water, one egg white and melted butter. Process until a firm, smooth dough forms. Turn out onto a work surface and knead into a ball. Wrap in plastic film and rest in the refrigerator for 20 minutes.

Preheat oven to 220 °C. Line three large baking trays with baking paper. Using semolina on the work surface to prevent sticking, cut the lavosh dough into 1 cm thick pieces. Using a pasta machine, roll the pieces of dough through the settings until approximately 3 mm thick. Cut the lavosh sheets to fit the length of the baking tray, allowing a little space between. Brush with the remaining egg white before baking in the oven for 10 minutes until lightly browned, puffed and crisp. Leave to cool on a cooling rack.

BLUEBERRIES

GLYNN JONES

A dedicated, die-hard Fremantle Dockers supporter, Glynn Jones left 'the big smoke' for a bush block just out of Northcliffe 21 years ago after a life-changing conversation with his young university-student neighbours. During a fishing trip, the students recounted an American lecturer's teachings about the future that included rising temperatures in the environment. South, Glynn concluded, was the direction to head.

Glynn is now the captain of the Northcliffe Fire and Rescue, and up until recently he had been the Pemberton Transfer Station (rubbish tip) caretaker for 12 years. Country tips inevitably become meeting places for blokes – unofficial 'Men's Sheds' where the important business of backyard sausage and wine making, local fishing and general local movements are discussed.

Moving from the bush block into town seven years ago after buying an established, small blueberry farm, Glynn now grows thirteen different varieties of blueberries that are in production from December through to March, depending on the weather.

Despite suffering with asbestosis as a result of being a refractory brickwork labourer for power stations and smelting factories in the Goldfields for many years, Glynn's vision is to restore his blueberry crop to full production. He manages the ever-damaging bird population with netting, and the weeds with guinea pigs, who have been trained to come on the call of the Dockers theme song!

Not yet able to supply into the Perth wholesale market, Glynn currently offers a pick-your-own blueberry experience, which is an annual tradition for many returning visitors staying in local accommodation over the Christmas holiday period. It's a highlight in the culinary year and especially so if you happen to also be a Dockers fan.

ELDERFLOWER BUSHES flower prolifically and make wonderfully light fritters, but if you don't have access to them, use fresh mint or pineapple sage leaves as an alternative.

ELDERFLOWER FRITTERS, SWEET LABNA & MULLED BLUEBERRIES

Sweet Labna & Mulled Blueberries

500 ml Greek yoghurt
1 cup red wine
½ cup sugar
1 cinnamon stick
5 cloves
5 whole allspice
¼ tsp cracked black pepper
1 bayleaf
1 sml orange, the peeled rind of
250 g blueberries
¼ cup (+ extra) icing sugar

Elderflower Fritters

200 g plain flour
300 ml (+ extra) cold sparkling water
1 sml free-range egg, beaten
a shot of grappa (optional)
vegetable or sunflower oil
6 lrg heads of freshly
picked elderflowers

SERVES 6

Place the yoghurt in a large piece of damp muslin (cheesecloth) material and hang to drain overnight in the refrigerator or in a cool place.

Bring the red wine, sugar, spices, bay leaf and orange peel to a gentle simmer. Simmer to reduce the volume by half before pouring over the blueberries in a small bowl. Loosely cover with a piece of baking paper and allow to cool before refrigerating overnight. The next day, drain the berries and simmer the spiced juice until syrupy. Pour back over the blueberries and leave to cool.

Take the yoghurt out of the cloth and combine with the ¼ cup icing sugar. Reserve in the refrigerator.

To make the elderflower fritters, sift the flour into a bowl and make a well. Whisk in the water and then the egg and grappa to make a thin batter the consistency of pouring cream. Allow to rest for 15 minutes before heating the oil in a deep pan to a depth of approximately 5 cm. Dip the flowers into the batter one at a time, shaking off the excess and gently lowering into the hot oil. Cook for a few seconds on either side before removing and draining on absorbent paper. Dust with icing sugar.

Place a dollop of sweet labna on the plate, pressing the back of the spoon in the middle to create a little depression. Spoon the blueberries onto the labna and serve with the elderflower fritters.

BROCCOLI

BRAD & ERIC IPSEN

Whether they love it or not, it's difficult to imagine children growing up without broccoli. Not so long ago it wouldn't have been considered as the green vegetable of choice for a family dinner; however, broccoli is now Australia's 10th largest vegetable crop in terms of value.

Brad Ipsen and his wife Sarah greatly enjoyed broccoli for the first time in the UK in the early 1990s and saw an opportunity to grow it on their Twin Lakes property at Perup, east of Manjimup. Brad's family had successfully grown cauliflower through the export boom and could see the market changing.

Twin Lakes is named after two large indented areas on the property. In theory, as they are in alignment with nearby Lake Muir, they were created by meteors centuries ago. Five German brothers settled the property in 1909 and they never married, retaining ownership until 1960 when the last of the brothers died. Two owners later, Brad's father, Eric, and mother, Louise, purchased the 900-acre property together with 700 acres further out in 1977.

Brad and Eric first grew broccoli in 1994 and they now grow six different varieties on a staged planting program throughout the year, except for six weeks from mid-March through to the beginning of May. Harvest starts at the beginning of August and continues until June. 'We've had to greatly increase production over the years and demand is still greater than we can supply,' Brad explains. 'Our record day for this past 2013 / 2014 season was 124 bins.'

Currently they supply 65% of their broccoli into Perth, 15% into Singapore and 20% to the eastern states. 'Export is still regarded as the golden goose; however, the high cost of production means our competitive edge is quality and industry integrity, which requires the support of all agricultural industries that equally can be challenged at any level,' Brad says in discussion about the future.

Along with growing broccoli, Brad and Eric also run 8,000 ewes of New Zealand Kelso sheep and 100 head of Angus Friesen cattle. All lambs are sold to the Western Australian Meat Marketing Co-operative Limited (WAMMCO International) in Katanning and get the benefit of grazing over harvested broccoli plants along with a managed pasture program.

With innovation and quality consistent factors in their future production and onsite packing facilities, Brad and Eric are looking to invest in vacuum cooling. This technology allows the Ipsens to quickly remove field heat from their broccoli, capturing freshness and providing longer shelf life.

Proving that karri are not the only successful 'green trees' in the Southern Forests region, Brad and Eric see a positive future in continuing to supply this in demand, delicious and versatile staple green vegetable – even if for some children this means only one branch at a time.

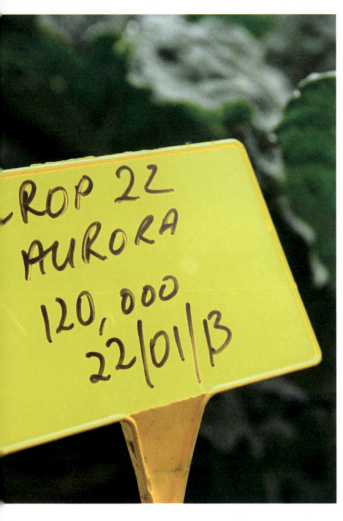

CROP 22
AURORA
120,000
22/01/13

BROCCOLI IS a very versatile vegetable that matches with many flavours. This recope is a side dish, but the addition of thinly sliced chicken breast or pork fillet when adding the leek and broccoli to the pan very quickly turns this into a delicious main.

SPICED BROCCOLI WITH LEEK, MUSTARD SEEDS, MACADAMIA NUTS, KAFFIR LIME LEAVES & CHILLI

2 tbsp vegetable oil

2 tbsp black mustard seeds

1 tsp ground cumin

1 tsp turmeric

2 – 3 small dried chillies

3 kaffir lime leaves

1 leek, the white part thickly sliced

2 sml or 1 lrg broccoli, cut into large long florets

salt flakes & freshly cracked black pepper

½ cup water

100 g macadamia nuts, roughly chopped

SERVES 4 AS A SIDE DISH

Heat the vegetable oil in a large deep frying pan, and on low heat gently fry the mustard seeds, cumin, turmeric, dried chillies and kaffir lime leaves for 1 minute. Add the leek and broccoli with a little seasoning and stir around in the spice mixture to coat. Pour over the water and cover with a lid. Cook for 5 minutes until the leek and broccoli are just tender. Remove the lid, cook a little further to allow all the moisture to evaporate before serving scattered with the macadamia nuts.

ZA'ATAR IS a Middle Eastern seasoning mix of dried thyme, sesame, sumac and salt that is used to finish a dish and can also be served as a dip in the same way as dukkah. The swirl of tahini sauce and the crunchy seasoning of the pine-nut za'atar elevates this simple broccoli soup to a whole different delicious level.

BROCCOLI SOUP WITH TAHINI, LEMON & PINE NUT ZA'ATAR

1 leek, roughly chopped

2 cloves garlic, roughly chopped

1 tsp sea salt

2 tsp ground cumin

2 tbsp olive oil

2 whole broccoli, heads & stems roughly chopped; reserving a few small leaves for garnish

1 ½ litres water or vegetable stock

1 x 400 ml can coconut cream

1 clove garlic, whole

½ tsp salt

½ tsp ground allspice

1 tbsp pine nuts

4 tbsp tahini

¼ cup lemon juice

2 tbsp water

2 tbsp extra virgin olive oil

salt flakes & freshly cracked black pepper

¼ cup pine nuts, lightly toasted

2 tbsp za'atar

SERVES 4

In a medium-sized pot, gently fry the leek and garlic, together with a teaspoon of salt and the ground cumin, in the olive oil until softened. Stir through the broccoli and then add the water or stock. Simmer for 10 to 15 minutes until the broccoli is soft. Puree together with the coconut cream until smooth and season to taste. In a large mortar and pestle, crush the whole clove of garlic together with the ½ tsp salt, allspice and pine nuts until a thick paste. Using a spoon, mix in the tahini, lemon juice, water and extra virgin olive oil to make a creamy sauce. Season to taste. Mix the toasted pine nuts together with the za'atar. Serve the soup drizzled with a little of the tahini sauce and garnished with a small broccoli leaf, along with a small dish of the pine nut za'atar.

BUCKWHEAT

JOHN DELLA FRANCA

Long before interest in protecting agricultural biodiversity and food traditions sparked the international Slow Food movement, the people of Tirano, in the Valtellina Alpine region in northern Lombardy, Italy were growing buckwheat. With little opportunity for prosperity after the Second World War, several families, including the Della Franca's, migrated from the Valtellina to the Southern Forests region.

After milling timber for several years, Joe Della Franca and his wife Elsie bought a 380-acre farm 4 km south of Pemberton to grow potatoes, raise beef cattle and continue with their culinary practices including the growing, harvesting and preparation of buckwheat.

Their youngest son, John, now undertakes this yearly tradition, growing approximately 5 acres of buckwheat using adapted equipment, and undertaking the laborious hand sorting of seed for the following year, discarding the 'wild' seed to keep the strain and quality pure.

Having no relationship to the wheat family, buckwheat is a cereal of the same genus as rhubarb, sorrel and dock. The first written evidence of buckwheat cultivation was in south-west Asia approximately 6000 B.C. The Crusaders got it from the Saracens, where it was given the Arabic-derived name 'Saracen Corn', and brought buckwheat into Italy and France via Russia and Eastern Europe.

Historically, buckwheat was associated with poverty, but in recent years it has had a revival due to its high nutritional value and its taste. Rich in fibre and silica, buckwheat contains a bioflavonoid called rutin, which is known to reduce high blood pressure. Either ground into flour or used as a grain in a similar way as rice, buckwheat contains no gluten and has a smoky earthy flavour with a slight bitter aftertaste.

There are many traditional dishes from around the world in which buckwheat is made, including: pizzoccheri (a buckwheat pasta, potato and cabbage dish) and taragna (buckwheat polenta) from the Valtellina in Italy; Japanese soba noodles; blini (a Russian yeast-leavened pancake eaten with sour cream and caviar); thick breakfast pancakes with maple syrup from North America; and kasha, an ancient type of porridge from Russia and Eastern Europe. The word kasha is also a misnomer for the uncooked roasted buckwheat grain.

Despite the Della Franca's buckwheat not being a commercial enterprise, instead used solely for their own and other local Italian families' food traditions, its history and contribution to this richly diverse region is one of its great culinary attributes.

THE PASTRY base of this rustic recipe has a deliciously earthy flavour and is wholesome and sturdy enough for many other types of fillings. For example, in summer, you could substitute the kale for thinly sliced ripe tomatoes and zucchini, or in winter, the potato slices topped with caramelised onions. The possibilities are endless but as with pizza toppings, take a less is more approach for the best results.

BUCKWHEAT, POTATO & KALE GALETTE WITH FRESH CHEESE, SAGE & GARLIC

4 medium waxy-style
potatoes, washed

180 g wholemeal self-raising flour

70 g buckwheat flour

200 g unsalted butter, chilled
and diced

½ tsp salt

½ cup Greek yoghurt

2 bunches kale

3 tbsp vegetable oil

2 tbsp extra virgin olive oil

100 g fresh cow or goats' curd cheese
or drained ricotta

80 g unsalted butter

4 cloves garlic, thinly sliced

1 cup sage leaves

salt flakes & freshly
cracked black pepper

SERVES 4

Using a mandolin, thinly slice the potatoes. Place in a bowl, cover with cold water.

Place the flours, butter and salt in a food processor and pulse until the mixture resembles coarse breadcrumbs. Add the yoghurt and continue to pulse until the dough just begins to combine. Turn out onto a lightly floured work surface and gently compress the dough together into a flattened ball. Wrap in plastic film and refrigerate for 15 minutes.

Cut the ribs from the kale leaves, slice thinly and then roughly chop the kale leaves. In a large pot, heat the oil until smoking hot and quickly fry the kale ribs and leaves until just wilted. Tip into a bowl and reserve to the side to cool. Drain the potato slices and evenly spread over a tea towel. Roll up the tea towel to extract as much moisture from the potato as possible.

Preheat oven to 200 °C. Roll the pastry out to a rough circle approximately 40 cm in diameter. Gently slide onto a large baking paper-lined baking tray. Leaving a 5 cm border around the edge, evenly layer the potato slices over the pastry and then top with the wilted kale. Drizzle with extra virgin olive before baking in the oven for 35 to 40 minutes until the pastry edges are golden, puffed and crispy. Place small spoonfuls of the fresh cheese over the kale.

Heat the unsalted butter in a frying pan until nut brown and fry the garlic and sage leaves until golden and crispy before spooning over the galette to garnish and serving with some salt flakes and freshly cracked black pepper.

BUCKWHEAT WAS introduced to Brittany in the west of France in the 12th century where it thrived on the harsh rocky landscape and, over time, both savoury and sweet crêpes made with buckwheat flour have become a tradition. Although not a traditional filling, this spiced apple butter makes a wonderful alternative to jam.

BUCKWHEAT CRÊPES WITH APPLE BUTTER & DOUBLE CREAM

Buckwheat Crêpe Batter

500 ml full cream milk
1 tbsp sugar
¼ tsp sea salt
80 g butter, melted
70 g buckwheat flour
100 g plain flour
3 large free-range eggs
butter, for frying

Apple Butter

1 kg apples, peeled, cored & thickly sliced
1 cup water
2 cups raw caster sugar
1 tsp ground cinnamon
½ tsp ground ginger
½ tsp ground nutmeg
¼ tsp ground cloves
½ tsp salt
double cream, to serve

SERVES 6

BUCKWHEAT CRÊPE BATTER

Whisk all the ingredients together until smooth. Cover and chill overnight. Remove the batter from the refrigerator about an hour before cooking. Stir to loosen the mixture, which should be the consistency of heavy cream. Add a little milk if too thick. Using a non-stick or crêpe pan drop a tiny piece of butter in the hot pan and wipe it around with a paper towel. Lift the pan and pour ¼ cup of the batter in the middle of the hot pan, swirling the pan to distribute the batter quickly and evenly. The pan shouldn't be too hot or too cold. After about a minute, run a thin spatula around the underside of the rim of the crêpe and then flip the crêpe over. Cook on the flip side for about 30 seconds, then slide it out onto a dinner plate. Repeat, cooking the crêpes with the remaining batter, stirring the batter every so often as you go.

APPLE BUTTER

In a medium-sized saucepan, combine apples and water. Bring to a boil, reduce heat to very low and simmer until apples are soft. Pass the puree through a sieve or food mill. Mix the strained puree with the sugar, spices and salt. Place sweetened pulp in a medium-sized saucepan and cook over medium-low heat, stirring frequently until thick.

TO SERVE

Place a dollop of apple butter in the middle of the crêpes with a dollop of double cream and fold them in halves twice and serve.

CAULIFLOWER

GARRY, IAN & JOHN RYAN

Mark Twain, the American author and humourist who wrote *The Adventures of Huckleberry Finn* in 1884, had this to say about a cauliflower, 'Training is everything. The peach was once a bitter almond. Cauliflower is nothing but a cabbage with a college education.'

Brothers Garry and Ian have farmed cauliflower and other various vegetables with their father John Ryan at their Cosy Creek farms north-east of Manjimup for most of their lives. John's father, the legendary Doc Ryan of Pemberton, purchased 1,400 acres of bush for his three sons in the early 1950s. After clearing the land in several stages, they initially started with dairy, apple orchards and potatoes.

'Cauliflower was only a winter crop then, but varieties and farming technology changed, enabling us to farm cauliflower 12 months of the year,' explains Garry. 'We have cool nights in summer, which allows us to successfully grow during the warmer months. The temperature drops below the 21 °C limit needed for brassicas' daily chill hour requirements, which means very few places can compete with us on quality during the summer period.'

During the 1980s and 1990s, cauliflowers were a booming export industry, with the majority being sold into the Singapore and south-east Asian markets. 'We couldn't grow enough,' Garry recalls. At its peak, Manjimup Fresh Produce, which is a co-operative of seven growers known then as MVeg, was the major packer of cauliflowers in the area and at the time exported 85% of all the cauliflowers sent out of Australia. Approximately 85% of those came from the Ryan and Edwards families.

The trade collapsed when the Chinese entered the marketplace in 2001 and the value of the Australian dollar increased. Today, 99% of Garry, Ian and their father's now more diversified vegetable crops are for the local fresh and vegetable-processing markets.

'We farm in big rotations in segregated smaller blocks, which have large areas of natural bush that act as a break for pests who don't like travelling through it. Completing irrigation by 2 pm in the afternoon also allows our brassicas to dry out by the evening, which prevents fungal problems.'

With developing better farm management techniques over the past 20 to 30 years that have included leaf testing and balancing the nutrients available in the soil to keep their plants healthy, Garry says they've not had to use chemical fungicides for the past 5 to 10 years.

Garry also attributes the region's clean air, good quality water supply and fertile soils as the major reasons they're also able to maintain high standards of quality in all of their brassicas. Everything a college-educated cabbage needs to be the best.

CAULIFLOWER CHEESE is an old favourite for many, but often doesn't present in the most appealing way. Serving the whole cauliflower to be cut in wedges at the table is a far more spectacular option.

CAULIFLOWER CHEESE WITH CARAWAY SEEDS

1 cup fresh breadcrumbs
olive oil
50 g butter
1 tbsp caraway seeds
4 tbsp plain flour
500 ml full cream milk
100 g strong cheddar cheese
1 whole large cauliflower
1 tbsp fresh thyme, finely chopped
salt flakes

SERVES 6 AS A SIDE DISH

Preheat oven to 200 °C. Spread the breadcrumbs out on a baking tray and drizzle with a little olive oil. Bake in the oven for 10 to 15 minutes until golden, stirring every 5 minutes to ensure they're evenly browned.

Melt the butter with the caraway seeds in a heavy-based saucepan over a low heat and stir through the flour. Continue to cook until the caraway butter has absorbed the flour and appears crumbly. Slowly pour in the milk while whisking until smooth. Place the saucepan on a simmer mat with the heat on a low setting and gently simmer while periodically stirring for 10 minutes. Stir through the cheese until melted. Cover and reserve to the side.

Preheat oven to 220 °C. Bring a large pot of water to the boil and place either a bamboo steamer or a large colander over the top. Using a small paring knife, core out the thicker end of the cauliflower stalk and trim away the remaining leafy-ribs. Place the cauliflower inside the steamer and cover with a piece of baking paper and aluminium foil and then a lid to cover as completely as possible. Steam for 20 minutes until a paring knife easily cuts into the thickest part of the cauliflower. Remove the paper and foil and transfer from the steamer to a baking dish.

Pour the cheese sauce over the top of the cauliflower to cover and bake in the oven for 10 to 15 minutes until the surface is golden. Serve scattered with the toasted breadcrumbs, thyme and salt flakes.

CONTRARY TO popular perception, cauliflower can be prepared in many different ways. Here are just four out of endless possible flavour combinations.

CAULIFLOWER FOUR WAYS

Roasted Cauliflower with Thyme, Capers & Parmesan

1 sml cauliflower, cut into florets
extra virgin olive oil
2 tbsp baby capers, rinsed
½ cup parmesan cheese, finely grated
1 tbsp fresh thyme leaves
freshly cracked black pepper

**SERVES 8 AS PART OF A
SHARED-PLATE OR 4 AS
A SIDE VEGETABLE DISH**

Pickled Cauliflower with Caraway & Bay Leaves

950 g cauliflower florets
1 cup salt
1 litre apple cider vinegar
1 litre water
500 g raw caster sugar
¼ cup caraway seeds
6 fresh bay leaves

**MAKES MORE THAN ENOUGH TO SERVE
8 AS PART OF A SHARED-PLATE**

ROASTED CAULIFLOWER WITH THYME, CAPERS & PARMESAN

Preheat oven to 220 °C. Spread the cauliflower florets in one even layer on a baking tray. Drizzle with extra virgin olive oil before roasting for 20 to 30 minutes, turning the cauliflower over in 5-minute intervals to evenly brown. Mix together with the capers, parmesan and thyme before serving with freshly cracked black pepper.

PICKLED CAULIFLOWER WITH CARAWAY & BAY LEAVES

Place the cauliflower into a large bowl and sprinkle over the salt. Toss to evenly coat the cauliflower. Leave for a minimum of 1 hour. Tip into a colander and rinse under cold running water to remove all the salt. Bring the vinegar, water, sugar, caraway seeds and bay leaves to the boil, stirring to dissolve the sugar. Place the cauliflower in large glass jars and then pour over the hot pickling syrup, ensuring the caraway is evenly distributed throughout the cauliflower. Leave for a minimum of 3 days before serving. RECIPE CONTINUES >

Fresh Cauliflower with Salad Burnet, Lemon & Dill

¼ cup extra virgin olive oil

1 tbsp lemon juice

sea salt flakes & freshly cracked black pepper

½ fresh cauliflower, thinly sliced using a mandolin

1 cup salad burnet or Italian parsley leaves

1 sml lemon, zested

¼ cup fresh dill sprigs

SERVES 8 AS PART OF A SHARED-PLATE

Cauliflower Fritters with Celery Salt

1 tsp celery seeds

2 tbsp salt flakes

½ cup chickpea flour

¼ tsp baking powder

½ tsp ground cumin

½ tsp turmeric

¼ tsp chilli powder

¼ tsp salt

200 ml water

peanut or vegetable oil, for frying

1 sml cauliflower, cut into small florets

SERVES 8 AS PART OF A SHARED-PLATE

FRESH CAULIFLOWER WITH SALAD BURNET, LEMON & DILL

Place the oil, lemon juice and a little seasoning into a small screw-top jar and shake to combine. Put the thinly sliced fresh cauliflower in a bowl and toss with the salad burnet leaves, lemon zest, dill and dressing until well coated. Serve with a little extra freshly cracked black pepper.

CAULIFLOWER FRITTERS WITH CELERY SALT

Grind the celery seeds in an electric spice mill until a fine powder. Mix together with the salt flakes until well combined. Store in an airtight jar.

Mix the chickpea flour, baking powder, ground cumin, turmeric, chilli powder and salt together in a bowl and stir through the water to make a pancake-batter consistency.

Heat a 3 cm depth amount of peanut oil in a deep frying pan or wide pot. Dip the cauliflower florets in the batter until well coated and then fry in the hot oil until a deep golden colour. Drain on paper towels before serving hot, seasoned with celery salt.

CHERRIES

GEORGE GROZOTIS

Despite all of the advancements in agriculture, the one element that's still elusive, uncontrollable, and yet crucial to naturally producing quality food, is the weather. Arguably, cherry growers are among the most vulnerable to Mother Nature's kindness and fury, working hard to produce one of the most anticipated fruits in the seasonal and festive calendar.

George Grozotis has been growing cherries on his Cherry Lane Fields property in Manjimup since he was a boy. George's father was the child of Macedonian migrants, who cleared the land during the 1940s to initially grow tobacco. After the tobacco finished in 1961, George's father planted 10 acres of apples, followed by another 25 acres of apples and 100 cherry trees in 1964.

'Years ago we had a small block of cherries alongside the apples that were the magnificent white-fleshed Napoleon variety,' George explains, 'it had the best flavour of all the cherries, but was highly susceptible to nose splitting and wind blush, so it unfortunately wasn't acceptable to the cosmetic and specific-size-driven marketplace.'

Fortunately, though, the newer varieties such as Simone, Lapins, Sweetheart and Sweet Georgia haven't gone the same way as the modern varieties of other highly perishable fruits – strawberries and tomatoes. 'I don't know where we're going with that,' George laments, 'the older varieties always delivered flavour even if they were more difficult to grow.'

George now manages 10,000 cherry trees, with 16 different varieties planted over 12-½ hectares. The earlier, more thin-skinned, varieties generally start ripening at the end of November, with the tastier varieties ripening after Christmas. George supplies 70% of his production to Woolworths with the remaining going to independent grocers and private shops.

Cherry trees also require the pollinating work of bees, so George has in recent years managed 30 of his own hives. 'I'm 60 years old and still love farming and now also the bees. I'm always learning something and will keep working for as long as I'm physically able.'

The most recent advancements in cherry growing are the use of biological controls that assist with delaying ripening, allowing George to better stagger the harvesting schedule, and using natural products such as milk powder, which helps prevent fruit split. 'Milk powder has everything in it a tree needs. It not only saves the crop but feeds it as well!'

Manjimup has long been synonymous with cherries, celebrating the harvest with the Manjimup Cherry Harmony Festival at the beginning of December annually. The festival places the cherry at its centrepiece of a regional produce showcase, providing growers such as Cherry Lane Fields with the acknowledgement and reward they deserve for the gamble they take with Mother Nature each year.

A CLAFOUTIS is a warm fresh pudding made with a pancake-like batter that's of French origin. A classic dessert that's wonderful each cherry season.

CHERRY, ALMOND & KIRSCH CLAFOUTIS

3 free-range eggs
5 free-range egg yolks
350 ml cream
150 g caster sugar
100 g almond meal
15 g rice flour
1 tbsp melted butter
15 fresh cherries, destalked, pitted & halved
1 tbsp kirsch (optional)
icing sugar
10 fresh cherries, to garnish
Bannister Downs Whipping Cream, to serve

SERVES 6

Preheat oven to 180 °C. Beat the eggs, yolks, cream and sugar together in a medium sized bowl before whisking in the almond meal and rice flour until well combined. Transfer to a jug, cover and refrigerate for an hour. Brush the bottom of a 20 cm shallow, heavy-based baking dish with melted butter. Evenly place the halved cherries over the base and then pour over the clafoutis batter. Bake 30 minutes until the middle is set. Drizzle over the kirsch and leave to cool slightly before dusting with icing sugar. Serve garnished with whole cherries and whipping cream.

THESE LOVELY little pastries are made even more interesting with a sprinkling of black sesame seeds, which are also known as nigella and most commonly seen on Turkish bread.

CHERRY & CINNAMON BUCKWHEAT PASTRIES WITH BLACK SESAME SEEDS

Filling

500 g cherries, pitted & halved
4 tsp arrowroot (tapioca starch)
5 tbsp caster sugar
½ tsp salt
1 tsp ground cinnamon

Pastry

300 g plain flour
70 g (+ extra) buckwheat flour
2 tbsp caster sugar
1 tsp salt
1 tsp ground cardamom
250 g unsalted butter, chilled & diced
100 ml chilled water

To Assemble

1 egg yolk
2 tbps milk
black sesame seeds

MAKES APPROX. 20

To make the filling, stir the filling ingredients together and gently heat in a small saucepan for 5 minutes until the cherries have softened. Transfer to a bowl and allow to cool before covering with plastic wrap and chilling.

To make the pastry, place the flours, sugar, salt, cardamom and butter in the bowl of a food processer and blend for a few seconds until the mixture is in very small pieces. Add the water and blend again until the pastry just starts forming into a mass. Transfer to a work surface and press the pastry together into a flattened disc. Cover with plastic wrap and chill for 20 minutes.

Preheat oven to 200 °C. Roll the pastry dough out to approximately 2 to 3 mm thick and cut out 8 cm diameter discs using a round cutter. Place half the discs on a baking paper-lined baking tray.

Beat the egg yolk and milk together and brush around the edges of the pastry bases. Spoon a little of the filling onto the middle of each base, allowing a 1 cm border around the edge. Roll each remaining pastry circle out a little thinner before pressing on top of the bottoms. Press around the edges with the tines of a fork and then trim using the same round cutter.

Brush the tops of each pastry with a little egg wash before pressing four small holes into the tops using the fork. Sprinkle over a little black sesame and refrigerate for 15 minutes before baking in the oven for 20 to 25 minutes until golden brown.

CHESTNUTS, HAZELNUTS, WALNUTS & MACADAMIA NUTS

TONY FONTANINI

Being directly linked with agriculture, 'culinary tourism' is a new term for the old tradition of exploring local eating and drinking experiences when travelling. Fontanini's Fruit and Nut Farm is one of the Southern Forests' culinary tourism highlights during autumn. Unsurprisingly, this farm evolved due to the demand created by European migrants in the 1950s.

Located on Seven Day Road in Manjimup, the 65-hectare farm has been in the family since 1906 when Giovanni Fontanini migrated from Lucca in Tuscany, Italy and bought an adjoining farm to his brother Archimedes' property, now known as the heritage-listed Fonty's Pool. Years later Giovanni's son Neil realised the potential for nuts and replaced dead apple trees with chestnuts and walnuts, resulting in one of the most diverse fruit and nut orchards in the region.

Neil's son Tony, his wife, Shirley, and their son Shaun (who is now the fourth-generation) with his wife, Neysa, have continued with the Fontanini tradition since 1989 of an open-gate, pick-your-own experience between April and June. They offer autumn fruit such as apples, pears (including the now sought-after heritage variety Comice), feijoas and persimmons along with chestnuts, macadamias, walnuts and hazelnuts.

In earlier days, bus loads of European migrants travelled to Fontanini's from Perth, loaded their baskets and bags with produce before roasting the chestnuts on purpose-built hearths under an open-air gazebo; they ate, drank and sang traditional songs, enjoying the conviviality of gathering and celebrating an important seasonal treat.

Today the Fontanini family offers to roast the chestnuts in a brazier over a gas flame, which quickly produces that distinctive toasted, dark caramel, woody smell and sweet, earthy taste with the pleasantly crumbly texture of a good waxy potato.

There are several old buildings, including one the family used for making cheese, and about a third of the property is taken up with chestnuts, walnuts, macadamias and hazelnuts. Now that the buses of European migrants no longer arrive, one of today's challenges for the Fontaninis, who sell their nuts unprocessed, is to attract buyers willing to remove the outer shells – their own specialised natural packaging, however time-demanding and inconvenient.

In Italy, agritourism is a vital part of tourism experiences in regional areas, defined by the Italian Government under national law in 1985 as '…activities of hospitality performed by agricultural entrepreneurs and their family members that must remain connected and complementary to farming activities.'

For the Fontanini family whose origins lie in the heart of Italian hospitality and food culture, we can only offer hope and support to this wonderful generational business and regional asset.

CHESTNUT FLOUR was often used in place of or to extend a quantity of wheat flour in times of great poverty throughout Europe. Its delicious sweet taste can be used for many sweet and savoury dishes and is delicious combined with celeriac.

CHESTNUT PASTA RAGS, CELERIAC, MUSHROOMS & RADICCHIO

½ kg fresh chestnuts
200 g plain flour
55 g chestnut flour
½ tbsp extra virgin olive oil
pinch salt
7 free-range egg yolks
2 tbsp water
semolina, for dusting
1 med celeriac, peeled & cut into sml chunks
300 ml milk
30 g butter
2 cloves garlic, finely chopped
1 lrg field mushroom, thinly sliced
1 lrg radicchio, leaves separated and washed
250 ml cream
salt flakes & freshly cracked black pepper
1 cup parmesan cheese, finely grated

SERVES 6

Bring a shallow pan of water to the boil. Using a paring knife, make a shallow cut across the top of each fresh chestnut. Simmer chestnuts with a lid on the pan in small batches for 5 to 10 minutes. After removing with a slotted spoon, wrap in a tea towel to keep warm. Peel the outer husk and inner membrane from each chestnut using a paring knife.

Place the flours, extra virgin olive oil, salt, egg yolks and water in the bowl of a food processor and pulse until a stiff pasta dough forms. Knead on a clean work surface until the dough is smooth. Form into a ball, wrap in plastic film and rest in the refrigerator for 30 minutes. Cut 1 cm thick slices of pasta dough then roll through a pasta-rolling machine until 5mm thick. Sprinkle the pasta with semolina if a little sticky. Using a paring knife cut the long pasta sheets into approximately 3 cm wide strips.

Simmer the celeriac in the milk for 10 minutes until tender. Drain and reserve to the side, discarding the milk.

Bring a large pot of salted water to the boil and cook the pasta rags for 4 to 5 minutes until al dente. Strain, reserving a little of the cooking water.

Heat the butter in a large frying pan and gently fry the garlic for 1 to 2 minutes. Cook the sliced field mushroom in the garlic butter until tender. Add the peeled chestnuts, cooked celeriac and radicchio. Pour in the cream and a little of the reserved pasta cooking water and simmer until it just starts to become a little viscose. Season to taste. Fold through the pasta and serve with a generous sprinkling of parmesan.

THIS DELICIOUS savoury tart is made with Cambray Boursan, which is a fresh cows' milk cheese produced by Cambray Cheese 12 km from Nannup, and leeks that have been pre-cooked in verjuice and positioned on a crumbly short pastry made with ground hazelnuts. Use fresh goats' cheese if you're unable to purchase this lovely cheese.

LEEK, CAMBRAY BOURSAN & HAZELNUT SAVOURY TART

200 g unsalted butter, cold & diced
250 g plain flour
100 g ground toasted hazelnuts
½ cup sour cream or plain Greek yoghurt
2 medium leeks, the white part cut into 4 cm thick slices
30 g unsalted butter
½ cup verjuice or white wine
1 tsp fresh thyme, finely chopped
100 g Cambray Boursan or fresh goats' curd
4 free-range eggs
½ cup cream
salt flakes & freshly cracked black pepper
2 thyme sprigs, the leaves stripped & roughly chopped

SERVES 8

Make the pastry by processing the butter, flour and 50 g ground toasted hazelnuts in a food processor until the butter is roughly chopped and the size of a small fingernail. Add the sour cream and process until the dough has just started to form. Tip onto a bench, gather into a disc, wrap in plastic film and refrigerate for 20 minutes. In a small frying pan, gently poach the leek in the butter, verjuice and teaspoon of chopped thyme until just soft. Leave to cool. Preheat oven to 180 °C. Roll the pastry on a floured bench and line a 22 cm fluted loose-bottomed tart tin. Refrigerate again for 20 minutes before blind baking for 20 to 25 minutes. Scatter the remaining 50 g ground toasted hazelnuts over the pastry base before evenly positioning the leeks. Place spoonfuls of Cambray Boursan in between the leek. Beat the eggs and cream together with a little seasoning and gently pour over and around the filling. Scatter over the stripped thyme leaves and return to the 180 °C oven for 30 to 35 minutes until the custard is just set. Leave to cool for 10 minutes before serving.

THIS DENSE sturdy loaf is great to take along on a picnic or hike with or without whipped salted caramel butter; resistance, however, is futile! If dried pears are difficult to find, substitute with any other dried fruit of the same weight.

MACADAMIA & DRIED PEAR LOAF WITH WHIPPED SALTED CARAMEL BUTTER

Macadamia & Dried Pear Loaf

50 g rolled oats

180 ml milk

½ cup Greek honey yoghurt

240 g wholemeal self-raising flour

1 tsp baking powder

1 tsp ground allspice

150 g dried pears, chopped

75 g soft brown sugar

3 tbsp honey

1 lightly beaten free-range egg

100 g macadamia nuts, toasted & roughly chopped

Salted Caramel Butter

300 g caster sugar

4 tbsp water

240 g unsalted butter, cut into small pieces

200 g cream, warm

1 tbsp salt flakes

SERVES 12

MACADAMIA & DRIED PEAR LOAF

Soak the oats in the milk and yoghurt in a small bowl for 30 minutes. Preheat oven to 180 °C. Lightly grease and line a 20 cm loaf tin with baking paper. Place flour, baking powder and allspice into a bowl and stir in the rolled oats mixture, dried pears, sugar, honey, egg and 60 g of the macadamia nuts until combined. Spoon the mixture into loaf tin and sprinkle with the remaining macadamia nuts. Bake 30 to 40 minutes until a skewer comes away clean. Leave to cool.

SALTED CARAMEL BUTTER

Place the sugar and water in a saucepan, cook on low heat and stir until the sugar has dissolved. Increase to a high heat and boil until a deep golden caramel forms. Turn the heat off before adding the butter in three separate amounts, stirring after each addition. Stir through the cream until combined. Transfer to a bowl and leave to cool before refrigerating until completely chilled.

Place in a food processor and blend for 2 minutes until lighter in colour and texture. Return to the bowl and stir through the salt flakes.

TO SERVE

Serve slices of the Macadamia & Dried Pear Loaf generously spread with Whipped Salted Caramel Butter.

THIS FAMOUS and thoroughly addictive walnut tart from the beautiful Engadine region in Switzerland is traditionally eaten cold when the caramel has cooled and set after baking. Though, if you, like me, find it impossible to resist when those freshly baked nutty aromas waft through the kitchen, it can equally enjoyed warm when the filling oozes and the pastry shatters and crumbles.

SWISS ENGADINE WALNUT TART

Filling

400 g soft brown sugar
400 ml cream
400 g walnuts
2 tbsp honey
½ cup marmalade

Pastry

150 g icing sugar
375 g plain flour
pinch salt
225 g unsalted butter, diced & chilled
6 free-range egg yolks
seeds from 1 vanilla pod
1 free-range egg yolk
¼ cup milk

SERVES 12

Make the filling first by melting the soft brown sugar with a quarter cup of the cream in a medium-sized saucepan. When melted and bubbling, add the walnuts, rest of the cream and honey. Simmer for a few minutes until it starts to thicken a little. Pour into a bowl, cover and completely chill in the refrigerator.

To make the pastry, place the dry ingredients and butter in the bowl of a food processor. Process until the pieces are the size of a small fingernail. Add the yolks and vanilla seeds and continue to process until the dough starts to form but is not yet a mass. Turn out onto a floured bench, press together into a flattened disc, wrap in plastic film and rest in the refrigerator for 20 minutes.

Preheat oven to 180 °C. Cut one-third of the pastry off and reserve to the side. Spray a 28 cm x 3 cm deep loose-bottomed fluted tart tin with cooking spray. Roll the larger amount of pastry until 3 mm thick and gently transfer to the tin. Using your fingertips, gently ease the pastry into the bottom edge of the tin. Trim the pastry around the top rim, allowing for a 2 cm overhang. RECIPE CONTINUES >

Gently heat the marmalade and force through a fine sieve, discarding the solids. Evenly brush over the pastry base. Spoon the chilled filling into the pastry base and smooth the top. Fold the 2 cm pastry overhang onto the filling. Beat the egg yolk and milk together to make an egg wash. Roll the remaining pastry out to 3 mm thick. Brush the pastry edge lying on top of the base with a little egg wash and then brush the entire lid with the egg wash. Gently place the lid onto the filling with the egg wash side facing down onto the filling. Press around the edges to stick the lid to the pie base. Trim around the edge with a small knife. Using a fork, lightly press around the edge of the tart to ensure the lid sticks to the base. Brush the top with the egg wash before placing on a baking tray and baking in the oven for 45 to 50 minutes, until golden brown. Leave to cool for a minimum of 30 minutes before serving.

FEIJOAS

ROBERT TAYLOR

Experiencing childhood on a farm in the Southern Forests – taking in the smell of the mushroomy damp earth and freshly cut hay, and the sweet taste of fruit in season, while being surrounded by those mammoth lungs-of-the-earth karri trees – doesn't always lead directly to being a primary producer.

Robert Taylor's pathway to being a feijoa grower later in his life has been a kind of circling back to what he really loved most. 'I always wanted to grow something…so now when I've had enough of the shop I go out to the farm, take a deep breath of fresh air, cool off and let it all clean my mind,' reflects Robert.

After spending his childhood in Deanmill, working on local dairy farms and orchards on weekends and during school holidays, Robert undertook a four-year apprenticeship, qualifying as an electrician. He started his own business, Warren Electrical Services, in 1973 with his wife, Kathy, which now includes his two sons, Dean and Paul, and services the Southern Forests and surrounding areas.

In 1991 Robert and Kathy had the opportunity to buy an 80-acre farm in the old Group Settlement area of Yanmah, north-east of Manjimup, complete with a derelict apple orchard. He had two close friends in the horticulture industry, one a New Zealander who advised Robert to plant feijoas, and the other a respected local apple grower, who encouraged him to renovate the apple trees. Robert set about doing both, planting 98 feijoa trees in 2002.

Being aware that feijoas are a relatively unknown fruit in Australia and therefore a very niche market, Robert has patiently tended the feijoas and generously offered fruit to anyone interested in the hope that a demand will be created.

Feijoas are from the guava arm of the large Myrtaceae family of plants, which also includes the spices cloves, cinnamon, allspice, nutmeg and the Australian native genera Eucalyptus, Callistemon and Melaleuca. Surprisingly, the feijoa flower is very similar to a eucalyptus flower and the plant is often used as an ornamental garden hedging plant.

The egg-shaped fruit has a crinkly skin with the flesh best experienced when capped like a boiled egg and then squeezed and sucked directly into your mouth. The highly perfumed taste can best be described as a cross between pineapple, guava, apple and those old-fashioned musk lollies.

As the feijoas have thrived, so have Robert's apples, bearing fruit with remarkable colour and sweetness. Robert's horticulture friends set up trials to find out why his apples coloured so well and found his location was 10˚C cooler at night and 10˚C hotter during the day. That unique environmental aspect to the growing of quality fruit has also been proven in Robert's success with feijoas.

As retirement creeps closer, Robert will completely hand over his electrical business to his sons in favour of spending more time at his orchard, returning to his childhood love of the land and passion for growing fruit. 'You wouldn't do it if it was only about making money. The love of anything you do will always come through in the end product you produce.'

THE BEAUTIFUL pattern of a cross-cut piece of feijoa makes for a spectacular dessert when set in a jelly. The apple cider is a soft and lovely background flavour, which together with the damp woody scent of cloves and taste of roasted almond makes a wonderful match with the tropical guava-like taste of the feijoas.

FEIJOA & APPLE CIDER JELLY WITH TOASTED ALMONDS & CLOVE-INFUSED CREAM

4 titanium-strength gelatin leaves

2 x 330 ml bottles
Mountford Soft Cider

½ cup caster sugar

4 feijoas, peeled & thinly sliced

500 ml cream

1 tbsp whole cloves

1 cup almonds, toasted &
roughly chopped

½ tsp ground cloves

SERVES 6

Soak the gelatine leaves in cold water for 5 minutes to soften. Heat the cider and sugar together while stirring to dissolve the sugar. Squeeze the softened gelatine leaves to remove excess water and stir into the hot, sweetened cider. Pour into a jug and place in the refrigerator to cool. Lay a slice of feijoa in the bases of six individual glass moulds or jars and pour over a 1 cm depth of cider mixture. Refrigerate until set and then repeat another three to four layers. Leave for a minimum of 4 hours to completely set.

Heat the cream with the whole cloves and leave 4 hours to infuse. Strain and refrigerate.

Dip the glass moulds into hot water to release the edges of the jelly and turn out onto each serving plate. Pour the cream around the edge of the jelly and sprinkle with the almonds and ground cloves before serving.

FIGS & RUSTLEBERRIES

KAY & PHIL GRAVETT

Most of us are only familiar with the more common types of berries such as strawberries, raspberries, blueberries and mulberries, but varieties from the Rubus fruit family number in the thousands, thanks to their ability to interbreed and set seed without fertilization.

On purchasing their 16-hectare block in 2006, Kay and Phil Gravett discovered a possible cross between a blackberry and an old English raspberry on a bush with a resident tiger snake that 'rustled' away to the opposite side of the bush when approached. They saved it from the excavator and, being delighted with its fleshy sweetness and size, they called the berry 'Rustleberry' and their new property 'Rustlers'.

'Rustlers' is located near the old Yanmah town site that was an early part of the Group Settlement scheme to develop land predominately for dairy farming in the 1920s. English migrants, who were part of this scheme, brought out berries along with other plants and animals to Australia for their 'new farms' and although yet to be officially confirmed, Kay believes this hybridization is a possible legacy of this.

After advice from good friends in the local horticulture industry, and with extensive planning and renovating of the long abandoned site, Kay and Phil established half a hectare of trellising for the Rustleberries. They also planted several types of figs, including an unknown variety from cuttings of an ancient fig tree near Lake Muir they've called 'Rowley's' after Rowley Muir, a member of the early pioneering Muir family. They've also planted pomegranates, walnuts, chestnuts, olives and the d'Agen plum most commonly known as the sugarplum.

Being born into local farming families and with years of beef farming experience and a love of machinery, working 16 hectares after farming over 600 hectares is something they consider a hobby during retirement. Confessing to not being able to 'sit still', they also wished to provide a connection with country life and the opportunity for their grandchildren to see food grow.

'We keep getting told we're mad,' Kay says through a chuckle. Fortunately for the region, markets, and chefs in high-end Perth restaurants, Kay and Phil have continued with their hobby.

FIGS HAVE a fleeting season, so having a variety of ways to enjoy them in a short time is the best way to maximise this seasonal treat. The fat hen (Chenopodium album) in this salad is a common weed that tastes similar to corn salad. Italian parsley leaves are a suitable substitute.

SMOKED DUCK, FRESH FIG, RICOTTA, PICKLED WALNUT, FAT HEN & RADICCHIO SALAD

2 x Holy Smoke smoked duck breasts or 1 lrg Holy Smoke smoked chicken breast, thinly sliced

1 lrg radicchio, the leaves washed & torn into bite-sized pieces

1 lrg handful fat hen or Italian parsley leaves

3 Pretsel Vineyard Pickled Walnuts, thinly sliced

1 cup fresh ricotta, drained

4 lrg fresh figs, quartered

4 tbsp fig vincotto or Balsamic vinegar

extra virgin olive oil

salt flakes & freshly cracked black pepper

SERVES 4

Layer the smoked duck slices, radicchio, fat hen and pickled walnuts on four plates. Top with small spoonfuls of fresh ricotta and then four quarters of fresh fig for each serve. Drizzle over a little fig vincotto and extra virgin olive oil and season before serving.

GUM MASTIC is a tree resin that is used as a flavouring in Greek sweet dishes. It has a pine and cedar like taste that is a wonderful match with cardamom and fresh fig. Sold in small crystals, it's available from specialised gourmet grocers or spice merchants.

MASTIC & CARDAMOM ICE CREAM, RUSTLEBERRY SORBET, GRILLED FIGS & WALNUT BRITTLE

Mastic & Cardamom Ice Cream

1 tbsp whole green cardamom pods
500 ml full cream milk
500 ml cream
1 cinnamon stick
¼ cup caster sugar
1 tsp gum mastic crystals
8 free-range egg yolks

Rustleberry Sorbet

1 kg frozen rustleberries
220 g caster sugar
2 tbsp lime juice

Walnut Brittle

1 cup caster sugar
1 cup light corn syrup
½ cup water
1 tbsp unsalted butter
1 ½ cups walnuts, coarsely chopped
1 ½ tsp bicarbonate of soda
1 tsp vanilla extract

Grilled Figs

12 fresh figs, halved
½ cup soft brown sugar

SERVES 8

MASTIC & CARDAMOM ICE CREAM

Lightly crush the cardamom pods in a mortar and pestle before combining with the milk, cream and cinnamon stick in a medium-sized saucepan. Just bring to a gentle simmer before turning off the heat and leaving to steep for 1 hour. Crush 1 teaspoon of the sugar together with the mastic crystals in a mortar and pestle until a fine powder. Whisk into the egg yolks together with the remaining sugar in a medium-sized bowl. Gently reheat the milk mixture before pouring and whisking into the yolk mixture. Return the custard mixture to the saucepan and place over the lowest heat possible, stirring continually while cooking until a thick enough consistency to coat the back of a spoon. Pour through a fine sieve into a large bowl and then cover the surface of the custard with baking paper. Chill in the refrigerator before churning in an ice cream machine.

RUSTLEBERRY SORBET

Defrost the rustleberries, reserving the liquid. This will provide 600 g thawed berries and 500 ml of thawed juice. Gently warm the juice and sugar together to dissolve. Puree the thawed berries before forcing through a fine sieve to remove the seeds. Whisk the puree together with the syrup and the lime juice. Chill in the refrigerator before churning in an ice cream machine.

RECIPE CONTINUES >

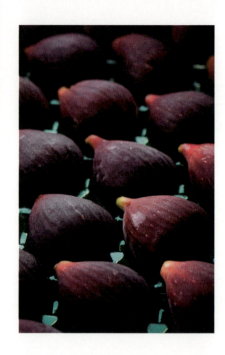

WALNUT BRITTLE

Line a large baking tray with baking paper coated with cooking spray. In a heavy-based medium-sized saucepan, heat the sugar, corn syrup, water and butter, stirring to dissolve. Boil until the syrup reaches 135 °C on a sugar thermometer and is a light golden colour. Stir in the walnuts and continue to cook for another minute. Remove from the heat, stir in the bicarbonate soda and vanilla and then quickly pour onto the prepared baking tray. Spread with a cooking spray–coated spoon to a 1 ½ cm thickness. Cool completely before breaking the brittle into small bite-sized chunks and crumbly texture.

GRILLED FIGS

Preheat a grilling element. Cut the figs in halves lengthwise and place on a baking paper–lined baking tray. Evenly sprinkle over the soft brown sugar. Place under the grill and cook until caramelised and softened.

TO SERVE

Place three grilled fig halves on the plate with a scoop each of the Mastic & Cardamom Ice Cream and Rustleberry Sorbet. Scatter over a little of the Walnut Brittle and serve immediately.

FINGERLIMES

ROB & JILL BAKER

The Australian demographic phenomenon of leaving or retiring from urban life for a perceived slower pace of living (called a seachange or treechange) has been a great contributing factor to the increasing diversity of small-scale primary producers in many regional areas around the country, including the Southern Forests.

Retired physiotherapists Rob and Jill Baker decided to purchase a small property 12 km from Pemberton near the Big Brook State Forest in 2002. With two empty paddocks, a love of food, and a desire to grow something a little different that was manageable and allowed them time throughout the year for other pursuits, the decision to grow native Australian fingerlimes was the result of a happy accidental internet search entry.

Native to the coastal rainforests of Queensland and New South Wales and enjoyed by early colonists, fingerlimes are shaped a little like a small pickled cucumber and grow up to 12 cm long, with a slight curve and textured skin-colour varying from dark mahogany brown and green through to rosy pink. When cut across, five or six longitudinal segments yield hundreds of compressed little beads (sometimes referred to as crystals) that have a similar appearance to caviar and burst with deliciously sweet-yet-acidic juice.

Removed with the same action as squeezing a tube of toothpaste, these juicy, tangy vesicles have been highly sought after by leading chefs for some years due to their unique popping texture in the mouth, perfumed citrusy taste and distinctive pearl-like visual appeal as a garnish.

In their native habitat, finger limes are very diverse and vary greatly in size, shape, colour and seediness. They can grow as a thorny understory shrub, or tree up to 6 metres high, on a range of soil types. All commercial fingerlime orchards have propagated cultivars in a variety of shapes and sizes.

Having planted their first fingerlime in 2006, Rob and Jill harvested their initial commercial crop in 2011 and sold out in a short time to Perth's top chefs. Pemberton's cooler summers and higher rainfall, and Rob and Jill's naturally wind-protected location, have contributed to this rainforest native succeeding where it has not been grown before.

Depending on the year, the season lasts approximately 6 weeks from around the end of March until around the end of April. Jill and Rob pick, sort, pack and dispatch the fingerlimes themselves together with their daughter Jacquie, who handles the sales and marketing. Their hands-on ability, and love of food and a country lifestyle, have contributed to realising their treechange dreams and given the region another unique addition to its ever-increasing offerings.

THE FINGERLIME beads are the jewels of this refreshingly light dish, providing the crunch and acid needed to balance the creamy avocado and sweet marron. This dish doesn't benefit from sitting around too long so prepare just before serving.

MARRON & AVOCADO CEVICHE WITH LIME, FINGERLIME & GARLIC CHIVES

4 x 150 – 200 g whole live marron
½ cup fresh lime juice
salt flakes
1 ripe avocado, peeled, stoned
& thinly sliced
¼ cup garlic chives, finely chopped
2 tbsp garlic chive or fennel flowers
¼ cup lime-infused extra
virgin olive oil
4 fingerlimes

SERVES 4

Place the marron in the freezer for 20 to 30 minutes, until they are very cold but not yet frozen. Bring a large stock pot of water to the boil and put the marron in quickly, placing the lid on the pot immediately, for 2 to 3 minutes. Drain and plunge the marron immediately into ice cold water. To remove the shell, twist the head off the body and discard. Hold the marron tail end in one hand with the underside facing upwards and, using kitchen scissors, cut down the middle of the soft, ridged shell from the top to the end of the tail. Using two hands, open the shell from cut side, releasing the marron flesh, which will still be partially raw. Carefully cut down the middle of the top side of the marron flesh and remove the alimentary canal. Rinse under cold water.

Slice the marron flesh into thin slices and place on a ceramic or glass platter. Pour over the lime juice and sprinkle over a little salt flakes. Leave for 1 hour. To serve, divide and layer the marron and avocado onto four plates. Drizzle over a little of the lime juice remaining on the platter. Scatter over the chopped garlic chives and flowers and then drizzle with the lime-infused olive oil. Cut the fingerlimes in halves crossways, squeeze to remove the caviar-like vesicles and scatter over the top to garnish.

GARLIC

DAVID MACDONALD & CATRIN IVERSEN

For some time, the alarm bells have been ringing about imported garlic – the bleaching, the chemicals and the nasty taste. However, it seems that irrespective of quality, the low cost has put a great deal of pressure on our own local suppliers over the years resulting in smaller growers exiting the industry. Fortunately for us, David MacDonald hasn't – but he's increasingly concerned.

There are many different varieties of garlic, which fall under two different types: soft-neck and hard-neck. Soft-necks can be braided, are the easiest to grow, produce larger bulbs and have higher yields but a simple taste. Hard-necks have fewer but larger cloves per bulb and have a better and more complex flavour. They can also produce bulbils, which are small cloves formed on top of the stem that are intensely flavoured and can also be used for planting. There is also the Elephant or Giant Russian garlic, which has a very large solid bulb and is more closely related to leeks.

David grows a delicious hard-necked variety called Italian purple that is planted between Anzac Day and Mother's Day. Although not certified, he chooses not to use any chemicals, preferring organic practices despite these methods being labour intensive.

After his rich karri loam soil is prepared, the single cloves of garlic are planted by hand in a particular direction ensuring bulb shape uniformity. Over the next seven months these rows are hand weeded, which in fertile country is a never-ending task undertaken by David and backpackers that live onsite throughout the year.

The garlic is ready in December, three weeks after the scape has shown, which is the long green shoot that rises from the base and is also an edible treat. After hand harvesting, they are hung in bunches to dry and then each bulb is cleaned and trimmed by hand. The clean bulbs are then stored in string bags awaiting packing and delivery.

David and his German partner, Catrin Iversen, started growing garlic as a secondary income three years ago. David's 400-hectare family property located west of Northcliffe was developed by his English and Scottish grandparents, who together with his parents have farmed dairy, pigs, seed and fresh potatoes, cauliflower, broccoli and beef, which he still grows today. His herd consists of 32 head of the prized Waygu, plus 170 beef breeders of various other types, and several Angus bulls.

This season, David and Catrin will plant up to 500 kg of seed garlic, aiming for a seven-fold weight return. As the harvesting period in the Southern Forests is later in the season due to its southerly location, they have found the timing a challenge. Suppliers in the north are able to fill the market earlier, commanding better prices. They will, however, continue to explore grower-direct options that will assist with taking out the regular, costly market-chain distribution process.

Smaller growers play an important role in providing more niche products that in turn contribute greatly to the culinary diversity of our local food culture. Consumer awareness as to the real cost of producing garlic will assist greatly in the longevity of growers such as David and Catrin. Although this must translate into buyers deciding to value quality over low prices, and supporting local over imported.

BAGNA CÀUDA is a traditional dish from Piedmont in the North of Italy that is served in a similar way to fondue and eaten in cooler weather. The dish greatly relies on the freshness of the accompanying vegetables and the quality of the garlic.

BAGNA CÀUDA WITH SPRING VEGETABLES

10 – 12 garlic cloves, peeled
full cream milk
20 sml canned anchovy
fillets in oil, drained
300 g unsalted butter, softened
200 ml extra virgin olive oil
100 ml pouring cream

Suggested Vegetables:
stringless green & yellow beans, baby radishes, baby carrots, celery hearts, cos lettuce hearts, witlof, boiled globe artichokes, fennel & asparagus

SERVES 6

Place the garlic cloves into a small saucepan and cover with milk. Simmer until the garlic is soft and the milk has reduced to a small creamy amount. Puree the garlic and anchovies into the reduced milk with a stick blender until smooth. Whisk the butter and olive oil into the puree, occasionally warming over a low heat while whisking to amalgamate. Add the cream, gently warm and then pour into a pre-heated ceramic dish. Serve on a platter surrounded by fresh seasonal vegetables.

GRAPE TOMATOES & BABY CUCUMBERS

SHANE YLIOFF

The first grape tomatoes were grown in Australia in the late 1990s. They're a cross between a Roma and cherry tomato, with a lower acidity, sweeter taste, slightly thicker skin and less 'squirt-power' when bitten into than a regular cherry tomato.

Shane Ylioff and his wife, Janine, and parents, Terry and Denise, have commercially grown grape tomatoes and baby cucumbers on their family farm in West Manjimup since 2002. Their small family business, which operates under the name 'Hygrow-West', sells 90% of their produce into Perth via the Canning Vale Markets and the remaining 10% locally to the IGA stores in Pemberton, Manjimup and Nannup and the Pioneer Store in Walpole.

Shane's great grandfather Nestor migrated from Macedonia in 1928 to what he imagined to be 'the land of milk and honey.' He started out in the Wheatbelt and, on finding neither milk nor honey, soon moved to Manjimup. Initially, he grew tobacco and then changed to dairy and beef cattle.

The remaining family, including Terry who was also born in Macedonia, came to Manjimup in 1955 to continue the family farm. Discouraged from agriculture, Terry worked as the service manager for Muir Ford in Manjimup for 36 years despite still retaining a love of the land.

With his father's encouragement, Shane set out on his own after undertaking an agribusiness degree, and working on various farms and a local seed nursery during the boom export cauliflower period. He started with four tunnels of cherry tomatoes and an old orange grader purchased from a grower in Harvey that he converted for sorting the smaller fruit.

After sterilising the tunnels and attending to maintenance during the winter, the Ylioff family now sow the grape tomato and baby cucumber seeds in a separate nursery tunnel in late July, planting seven weeks later at the end of September in bags of local jarrah sawdust, training and feeding the plants through a recirculating system until the end of the season the following July.

The tomatoes and baby cucumbers are picked in the morning, sorted, weighed and packed in the afternoon and then transported directly to Perth in the late afternoon.

Shane and Janine's five children, who range in ages from 8 to 19 years, have grown up seeing something that city children now have as a regular inclusion in their lunchboxes grow from seed to plate, tasting and appreciating truly fresh produce – one of the many wonderful legacies of a country childhood in the Southern Forests region.

THIS DISH is the taste of summer in a bowl. Tomato water is an intensely flavoured tomato juice that is strained from the solids. Leaving the green calyxes on the tomatoes greatly adds to the flavour as do these accompanying garnishes.

TOMATO WATER, TOMATO CONFIT, PRESERVED LEMON, AVOCADO, BASIL OIL & NIGELLA

Tomato Water

1 ½ – 2 kg very ripe fresh cherry or other variety of flavourful red tomatoes, calyxes left on

8 thyme sprigs

sea salt

SERVES 8

Basil Oil

2 cups tightly packed basil leaves

1 cup olive oil

½ tsp salt

MAKES APPROXIMATELY 200 ML

Tomato Confit

2 punnets yellow & red cherry tomatoes

4 cloves garlic, peeled & halved

12 thyme sprigs

extra virgin olive oil

salt flakes & freshly cracked black pepper

SERVES 4

TOMATO WATER

Puree the tomatoes with the calyxes left on in a strong blender until smooth. Transfer to a large saucepan with the thyme and gently simmer for 15 minutes. Filter through a damp muslin cloth, extracting as much water as possible. Discard the solids. Season with salt to taste and allow to cool.

BASIL OIL

Blanch the basil leaves in boiling salted water for ten seconds. Drain and run under cold water until the leaves have chilled. Gently squeeze to extract as much water as possible and then roll in a dry tea towel. Allow to air-dry for half an hour before pureeing together with the olive oil and salt. Filter though a damp muslin-lined sieve for several hours or overnight. Discard the solids.

TOMATO CONFIT

Preheat oven to 150°C. Place the tomatoes and garlic halves on a deep baking tray and scatter over the thyme. Pour over enough extra virgin olive oil to cover and bake in the oven for 30 to 40 minutes until the tomatoes have just started to collapse. Reserve 16 to 20 tomatoes for the following recipe. Store the remaining in a sealed container in the refrigerator. RECIPE CONTINUES >

To Assemble

1 preserved lemon quarter
2 cups tomato water
1 ripe avocado, thinly sliced
16 – 20 confit tomatoes
½ cup purple basil leaves, gently torn
¼ tsp nigella seeds
a few drops basil oil

SERVES 4

TO ASSEMBLE

Remove the flesh from the preserved lemon, rinse under cold water and thinly slice. Ladle the tomato water into four bowls. Place the avocado slices in the middle of the bowls followed by the confit tomatoes, preserved lemon slices and basil leaves. Serve garnished with a pinch of nigella seeds and a few drops of basil oil.

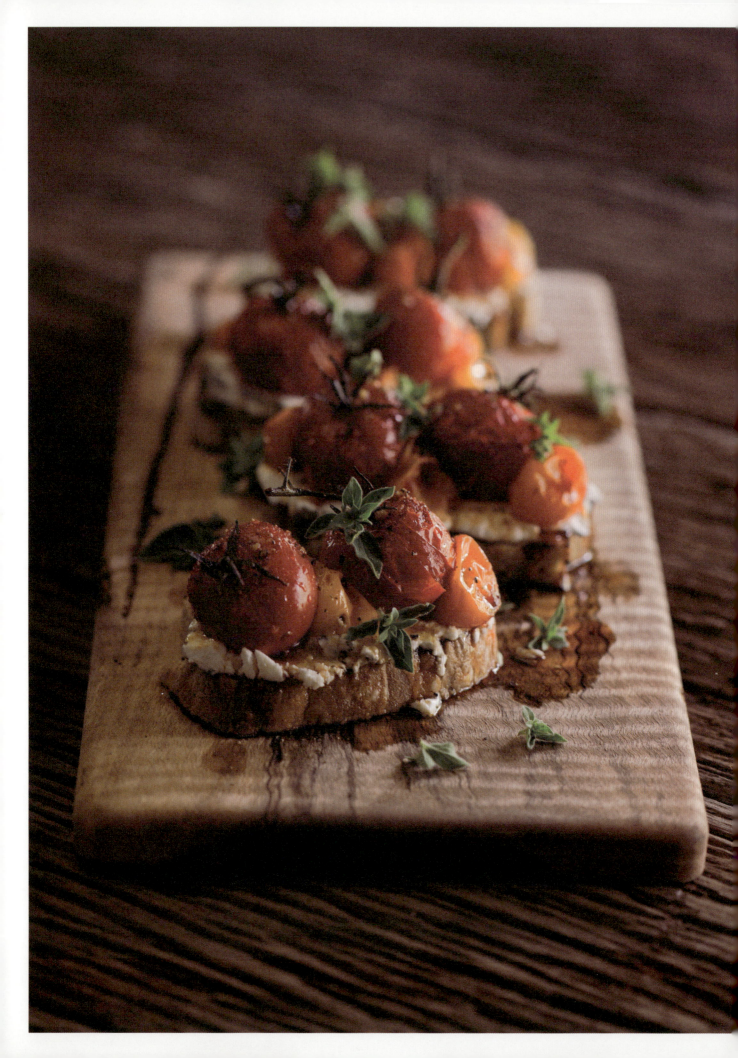

THE ADDITION of smoked paprika to roasted cherry or grape tomatoes adds an even greater depth of flavour to their wonderful sweetness.

ROASTED CHERRY TOMATOES, SMOKED PAPRIKA, ASHED GOATS' CHEESE ON GRILLED SOURDOUGH BREAD

2 punnets lrg red & yellow grape or cherry tomatoes

extra virgin olive oil

1 tsp smoked paprika

salt flakes & freshly cracked black pepper

4 thick slices sourdough bread, grilled or toasted

150 g fresh ashed goats' cheese

1 tbsp oregano leaves, to garnish

SERVES 4

Preheat oven to 220 °C. Place the cherry tomatoes on a baking tray and liberally drizzle with extra virgin olive oil. Sprinkle over the smoked paprika and season with salt flakes and freshly cracked black pepper. Roast in the oven for 20 to 25 minutes until caramelised but the tomatoes have still held their shape. Cut each slice of grilled sourdough in halves and thickly spread with the ashed goats' cheese. Top with the roasted cherry tomatoes, drizzle with the juices from the roasting tray and garnish with the fresh oregano leaves.

GREEN TEA

KATHY DAWSON

Walk into any café or restaurant now and it's rare not to see green tea included on the list of beverages. It can also sometimes be seen included in cakes, biscuits and desserts. Interest in green tea has increased worldwide in recent years as the health benefits have become more widely known.

Japan is a high-value market for Australian-grown green tea, and in 1997 the Department of Agriculture defined the Manjimup Pemberton area as having great potential to grow it. Kathy and Don Dawson, along with others, investigated the commercial opportunities of this new niche market. Meanwhile, the Department of Agriculture continued with trials and extensive research, identifying four or five varieties that flush at different times, thereby increasing the harvesting opportunities.

Being an acid soil–loving member of the Theaceae family of plants, green tea requires a cool climate with high-quality low-salt water, minimal days above 35 °C, and well-draining sandy loam.

Plants require four years to establish, after which their lifespan can reach up to and beyond 40 years. Irrigation and fertilisation are key factors in the quality of the tea, resulting in higher levels of antioxidant properties, which are highly sought after by pharmaceutical, cosmetic and food-manufacturing companies.

Another critical factor in producing high-quality green tea is the time between harvesting and processing. If steamed soon after harvesting, higher levels of a polyphenol and catechin EGCG, the powerful antioxidant thought to be active against cancer, are retained.

Kathy has a background in teaching but her great love of the land gave Kathy and her now late husband, Don, the desire to pursue this new industry. In 2007 they ordered the varieties Fushun and Sayamakaori, which they later planted on 1.3 hectares.

Currently, this new industry awaits the essential collaboration and financial support for a processing factory. The 50 hectares of green tea factored to make this viable have been deemed a very realistic prospect by those interested in this niche primary product; however, assurance that a processing facility will be in production by the time the harvest is ready is yet to be given, and that assurance is necessary for grower confidence and further investment.

Until then, plantations like Kathy's and others in the area, including the now established trial plot at the Manjimup Horticultural Centre, will continue to enjoy the soil, water and clean environment this region offers in abundance.

ICE CREAM sandwiches seem such a decadent treat whether they're made with biscuits or cake. The stunning green colour of the green tea ice cream certainly adds wow factor, and the earthy flavour of it works especially well with buckwheat, chocolate and cinnamon.

GREEN TEA, BUCKWHEAT, CINNAMON & CHOCOLATE ICE CREAM SANDWICH

Green Tea Ice Cream

1 tbsp matcha green tea powder
3 tbsp hot water
200 ml milk
200 ml cream
4 free-range egg yolks
5 tbsp caster sugar

Chocolate Buckwheat Biscuits

220 g unsalted butter, softened
110 g (+ ¼ cup) rapadura or raw caster sugar
110 g (+ extra) wholemeal flour
110 g buckwheat flour
2 tbsp cocoa
1 (+ ½) tsp ground cinnamon
pinch salt
2 tbsp milk
1 tsp vanilla extract
150 g dark chocolate, finely chopped

MAKES 8

GREEN TEA ICE CREAM

Combine the green-tea powder and hot water together in a bowl and reserve to the side. Combine the milk and cream in a saucepan and bring to a gentle simmer. Whisk the yolks and sugar in a bowl to combine and then pour over the hot milk and cream while whisking. Return to the saucepan and place over a very low heat. Continually stir with a wooden spoon and gently cook for 5 to 10 minutes until the custard is thick enough to coat the back of the spoon. Return to the bowl and whisk through the green tea powder paste to dissolve. Place a piece of baking paper directly on the surface before refrigerating until cold. Churn in an ice cream machine following the manufacturer's instructions.

CHOCOLATE BUCKWHEAT BISCUITS

Cream the butter and 110 g sugar. Add the flours, cocoa, one teaspoon of ground cinnamon and salt together with the milk and vanilla and combine until a soft dough. Transfer to a work surface and gently press into a rough flattened ball. Wrap in plastic and refrigerate for 20 minutes. Using a little wholemeal flour, roll the dough out to about 4 mm thick. Cut out 5 cm diameter rounds and transfer to lined baking trays, allowing a little space in between. Gather the scraps and re-roll until you've cut as many biscuits as possible. Refrigerate the biscuits for 10 minutes. Preheat oven to 180 °C. Bake for about 10 minutes until lightly browned. Combine the remaining ¼ cup rapadura sugar and ½ tsp ground cinnamon and sprinkle over the tops of the biscuits. Cool on trays. RECIPE CONTINUES >

Melt the chocolate in a bowl over just simmering water. Spread a little on the base of each biscuit and leave to cool, chocolate-side-up on a tray.

Place a scoop of green-tea ice cream onto the chocolate side of a biscuit and sandwich with another. Using a small palate knife, smooth the edges to fill in the gaps and create a neat edge. Place back in the freezer to set as you fill each biscuit. Serve sprinkled with a little more cinnamon sugar.

GREEN TEA and white chocolate are a wonderful flavour combination. These one-bite, sweet little filled shortbread biscuits were inspired by an edible gift from a Japanese friend, which was a much finer and more delicate version.

GREEN TEA, WHITE CHOCOLATE & ANISEED SHORTBREADS

Shortbreads

70 g icing sugar
1 ½ tbsp matcha green tea powder
150 g unsalted butter, softened
255 g (+ extra) plain flour
3 lrg free-range egg yolks
½ cup caster sugar
1 tbsp aniseed, lightly crushed

White Chocolate Butter Cream

150 g white chocolate
150 g unsalted butter, softened
160 g icing sugar
1 tsp vanilla extract

**MAKES APPROX. 50 SML
SANDWICHED SHORTBREADS**

SHORTBREADS

To make the Shortbreads, whisk the icing sugar and green tea powder together to combine. Cream the butter together with this mixture until fluffy. Gently beat in the flour and then the egg yolks until a soft dough forms. Gather into a flattened ball and wrap in plastic. Refrigerate for 30 minutes.

Preheat oven to 180 °C and line baking trays with baking paper. Using a little extra flour, roll the dough out to 5 mm thick and with a small scallop-edged biscuit cutter, cut as many biscuits out as possible. Combine the caster sugar and aniseed and lightly sprinkle over the biscuits, reserving a little. Chill for 10 minutes in the refrigerator before baking for 15 to 20 minutes until just starting to turn golden on the edges. Place on a wire rack to cool.

WHITE CHOCOLATE BUTTER CREAM

To make the Butter Cream, melt the white chocolate in a bowl over just simmering water. Remove from the heat and allow to cool to room temperature. Cream the butter, icing sugar and vanilla extract until fluffy. Slowly add the melted white chocolate until incorporated.

Sandwich the biscuits together with a little of this filling. Serve sprinkled with a little extra aniseed sugar.

HONEY

LEE FONTANINI

Keeping a beehive along with chooks and a vegie patch reflects Lee Fontanini's love of the natural environment and curiosity about its miraculous workings, with honey its delicious reward.

Being the granddaughter of Archimedes (Archie) Fontanini – one of Manjimup's founding Italian immigrant pioneers, whose enquiring mind, respect for the land and building skills resulted in the iconic Fonty's Pool – Lee has a deep connection with the Southern Forests region.

Lee lives on the edge of her grandfather's property, and has kept bees since 1994 when an English friend who used to make mead and use honey for various purposes got her started. The hives require time for maintenance four times per year, occasional observation and, when the hive has a good flow of honey, half a day every ten days for extraction. Lee can enjoy 30 to 40 kg of honey from each hive per year.

There are more than 1,600 species of native bees; however, European honeybees are more productive and therefore used for commercial production. There are three types of bees in a colony, which can have up to 60,000 bees at a time: sterile females that do most of the work; drones, which are males that attempt to mate with a virgin queen; and a queen.

A sterile female travels up to 10 km per return trip to collect pollen in baskets on her legs, and nectar, which is mixed with an enzyme and stored in a special stomach. When she returns to the hive, she passes the nectar to another bee through her mouth. This process is repeated and, when ready, it is deposited into the honeycomb cells. The bees then fan the honeycomb with their wings to evaporate excess water after which they seal the cells.

Aside from honey, bees produce beeswax to make the honeycomb cells in which to raise young, and store pollen and honey; propolis, a collected resinous mixture used as a sealant for small gaps in a hive; bee pollen, which is a mixture of pollen, enzymes, fungi and bacteria on which the female lays an egg; and royal jelly, which is a nutrient-dense secretion fed to bee larvae and adult queens.

Home beekeeping is best undertaken by first enquiring about your local council restrictions and undertaking some courses prior to compulsory registration with the Department of Agriculture and Food, and the branding of your beehive.

Unsurprisingly, bees consider a darkly clad moving person a threatening animal, which is why beekeepers wear white. The puffing smoker masks the bees' alarm pheromones and initiates feeding in case of abandonment due to a perceived fire, giving the bees full stomachs and slowing down their flexes to sting.

With 65% of commercial crops grown in Australia relying on bee pollination, it's vital for the productivity of farming and the security of food supply that our bees remain healthy and unaffected by the diseases and parasites that have crippled colonies in other countries.

If you're not interested in keeping bees yourself, local beekeepers need to be supported to ensure their viability. Independent beekeepers often travel great distances across our regions to ensure the supply of unique honeys as an alternative to mass-produced homogeneous blends.

Collecting honey is an ancient pursuit and its properties and flavour are a direct reflection of the plants and location where the bees collect nectar. This taste of place and miracle of nature are the elements that keep Lee and so many other backyard beekeepers fascinated.

THIS LOVELY dessert is a little like a deconstructed trifle minus the sherry. The different textures of the jelly, custard and madeleine deliver the nuanced flavours inherent in single-origin unblended honey in a delightfully interesting way.

HONEY & BAY LEAF CUSTARD, HONEY JELLY & HONEY MADELEINES

Honey & Bay Leaf Custard

600 ml Bannister Downs whipping cream
3 fresh bay leaves
5 free-range egg yolks
1 free-range egg
100 g local honey

Honey Jelly

1 titanium strength gelatine leaf
125 g local honey
2 tbsp honey mead or sweet wine
2 tbsp water
1 tsp lemon verbena or lavender flower tips (optional)

Honey Madeleines

3 free-range eggs
100 g caster sugar
1 lemon, the zest finely grated
100 g (+ extra) plain flour
1 tsp baking powder
100 g (+ extra) unsalted butter, melted
1 tbsp local honey (fluid consistency)
icing sugar, to dust

SERVES 8

HONEY & BAY LEAF CUSTARD

Bring the cream and bay leaves to a gentle simmer, remove from the heat and leave for 30 minutes to infuse. Preheat oven to 140 °C. Whisk the egg yolks, whole egg and honey together in a bowl. Reheat the infused cream and then pour into the egg mixture while stirring to combine. Transfer through a sieve into a jug, discarding the bay leaves, and then pour into eight small glass jars or ramekins. Place the filled jars into a deep roasting dish with a flat base and pour enough hot water into the pan to come halfway up the sides of the jars. Bake for 20 to 30 minutes until the custards have a loose, but set, wobble. Remove from the pan and allow to cool before refrigerating.

HONEY JELLY

Soften the gelatine leaf in a bowl of cold water. Combine the honey, mead and water in a small saucepan and bring to a gentle simmer while stirring. Squeeze the water out of the gelatine leaf and stir into the honey mixture to dissolve. Leave to cool before pouring a thin layer of jelly over each chilled custard and sprinkling over a little of the lemon verbena flowers. Leave for a minimum of 2 hours to set. RECIPE CONTINUES >

HONEY MADELEINES

Preheat oven to 190 °C. Brush 2 x 12 madeleine mould trays with melted butter. Leave the butter to set for a few minutes before dusting with flour, tapping the tray upside down to remove any excess. Whisk the eggs and sugar with an electric mixer until pale and thick. Whisk in the lemon zest. Sift the flour and baking powder together and gently fold into the egg mixture, followed by folding in the melted butter and honey. Chill this mixture for 15 minutes. Fill each of the madeleine moulds three quarters full and bake for 10 minutes until puffed and golden. Leave to cool for a few minutes before carefully removing from the tins.

TO SERVE

Dust the honey madeleines with icing sugar and place next to the honey and bay leaf custards with honey jelly.

JAM

BETH SHORTHOUSE

The lovely idea of growing her own fruit and vegetables during retirement has given Beth Shorthouse much more than seasonal freshness on her table. Making jam to preserve the excess has resulted in a 4,500-jars-per-year task that she accomplishes solo in her home kitchen, distributing her products to cafés and tourism outlets around the region and selling them at her bi-weekly stall at the Manjimup Farmers Market.

Beth and her husband John moved to their 42-acre property in the Middlesex Valley, 8 km south of Manjimup, in 1987 after 20 years of being transferred around Western Australia as government school teachers. 'We wanted our own piece of dirt,' Beth recalls. 'We were on Cocos Island for 12 months teaching and wanted to settle after 20 years of moving from place to place.'

Their property 'Yallamurrup', which means 'hill with a view' in a local Indigenous language, was originally a Group Settlement base known as 'Brucedale'. Their weatherboard home was the original club manager's house in nearby Nyamup, and, like many dwellings in the area, was transported in two pieces and reconstructed on site.

Continuing to teach in Manjimup after settling, Beth officially retired in 1999 but taught and tutored French part-time while John developed their vegetable garden and berry patch. In 2000, the beginnings of a local farmers market gave them an opportunity to sell their fresh produce, and provided another outlet for Beth's value-adding jams and sauces.

During a trip to the UK, France and Scotland in 2001, Beth was inspired seeing and tasting exciting new flavour combinations in the many farm shops and teahouses they visited. This allowed her to develop her range and expand her business using produce from other local growers in addition to their own.

In 2003 the Manjimup Farmers Market formed a management committee, with Beth volunteering as secretary, a role she still undertakes today. The region's small population, spread of growers over the large geographical area and, for many years, lack of suitable permanent market location, have presented many challenges to the longevity of the market. However, Beth's commitment to the market's operations and her stall within it have contributed to its survival and, of course, seasonal offerings.

Retirement has certainly been a misnomer for Beth and John; however, Beth maintains she wishes to remain a cottage industry, staying a single hands-on producer of preserves from their own garden and other local growers'. 'We love what we do and our small piece of paradise, so while we're still fit and we have a purpose to get up for each day, there's no reason to stop.'

TO THE uninitiated the idea of eating cheese and jam together is odd, but after eating this combination hopefully you'll change your mind. Bisciola is a special fruit bread that is traditionally eaten in the Valtellina region in the north of Italy at Christmas and also during autumn. The addition of buckwheat and rye flours gives it a wonderfully nutty flavour and is a typical inclusion in Valtellina, from where many families migrated to Pemberton.

SHEEPS' CHEESE, SPICED WALNUTS, BETH'S FIG JAM & BISCIOLA BREAD

Bisciola Bread

2 tsp dried yeast

3 tbsp (+ 1 tsp) caster sugar

600 ml warm milk

150 g buckwheat flour

150 g rye flour

300 g plain strong flour

1 tsp salt

¼ cup pine nuts

1 cup walnuts, roughly chopped

3 tbsp unsalted butter

2 free-range egg yolks

15 dried figs, stems removed & roughly chopped

¼ cup milk

MAKES 2 LOAVES

Spiced Walnuts

1 tbsp honey

2 tsp olive oil

2 tbsp soft brown sugar

1 tbsp water

2 cups walnuts

1 tsp sea salt flakes

1 tsp garam masala

½ tsp ground coriander

¼ tsp dried chilli flakes (optional)

SERVES 6

BISCIOLA BREAD

Dissolve the yeast and 1 tsp caster sugar in half a cup of the warm milk and leave 10 minutes until frothy. Place the flours, 3 tbsp caster sugar, salt, nuts, butter and one of the egg yolks in the bowl of an electric mixture. Using a dough hook beat slowly while adding the remaining warm milk until the dough starts to form. Add the figs and continue to slowly beat until the figs are incorporated. Turn out onto a lightly floured work surface and gently knead for 5 to 10 minutes. Divide into two and form two oval-shaped loaves. Place on a baking paper–lined baking tray and cover with plastic film. Leave for an hour to rise. Preheat oven to 200 °C. Beat the remaining egg yolk with ¼ cup milk to make an egg wash. Brush the two loaves with the egg wash before baking for 20 minutes. Reduce the temperature to 180 °C, turn the trays around and bake a further 20 minutes. Leave to cool on a cooling rack.

SPICED WALNUTS

Heat the honey, oil, sugar and water over medium heat until dissolved. Add the walnuts and toss to coat. Sprinkle the salt, garam masala, ground coriander and dried chilli over the nuts and toss until the nuts are well coated and lightly browned. Transfer to a baking sheet, spreading out to cool completely.

RECIPE CONTINUES >

To Serve

⅓ cup Spiced Walnuts

¼ cup fig jam

80 g matured sheeps' cheese,
roughly sliced

1 fresh fig

2 – 3 whole fresh walnuts in the shell

2 – 3 slices Bisciola Bread

PER PERSON

TO SERVE

Place the Spiced Walnuts and fig jam bowls in the middle of a serving platter. Surround with small piles of the accompanying sheeps' cheese, fresh figs, whole walnuts with nut cracker and slices of Bisciola Bread.

KIWIFRUIT & TAMARILLO

RUSSELL DELROY

The saying 'needs must' couldn't ring truer for how the kiwifruit and tamarillo became popular in New Zealand. Due to diminished imports as a result of the reduced shipping trade during the Second World War, New Zealand had to produce its own fruit throughout the winter. Kiwifruit and tamarillos thrived and filled this need and have since been popular fruit there – the kiwifruit now a well-known major commodities export.

In 1987, Russell Delroy saw an opportunity to replace the New Zealand kiwifruit and tamarillos coming into Australia. In the winter of 1988 he started out by planting 4 hectares of kiwifruit, 2 hectares tamarillos and 2 hectares of avocados in Pemberton, which had a similar climate and the same number of chilling hours and rainfall to the Bay of Plenty in New Zealand.

Born and raised on a wheat and sheep farm in Esperance, Russell moved to New Zealand with his parents, who went there to semi-retire while he studied horticulture at Massey University. Recognising the potential for horticultural diversity in the Southern Forests region and the opportunities for centralised packing and marketing, Russell returned to Australia and established Delroy Orchards in Pemberton. The packing and marketing side of the business is now located in Donnybrook and handled two-thirds of Western Australia's entire avocado production in 2013.

The kiwifruit and tamarillos have remained a smaller component of Delroys, with New Zealand still the global giant for kiwifruit, and tamarillos remaining a niche market due to their unfamiliar uniquely sweet and acidic taste. 'The majority of our tamarillos go to the restaurant trade, high-end gourmet grocers and have a cult following from the expat New Zealanders. In the past when we've given tasting samples, the majority of those who love the taste are children,' Russell explains.

Russell now has 10 hectares of kiwifruit, 10 hectares of tamarillos (the largest plantation in Australia) and 180 hectares of avocados. These have been managed by local ex-cauliflower grower Rob Dimetriou for the past ten years, who has a work ethic and dedication to growing quality local fruit as if it were his own.

Asked what sets this region apart from others in terms of its growing conditions, Russell explains that it's about the diurnal temperature variation, 'having the chill hours at night time gives the product a rest, reinforcing, tightening and creating smaller cells in the plant which assists with growing a higher quality, better tasting and fresher product that lasts longer.'

Given the advanced transport networks and technology for storing fruit that enable the provision of quality fruit long after the last apple has been picked, it's safe to assume that tamarillos and kiwifruit won't be the only fruit in the bowl in June, July and August. However, in terms of this fruit providing a unique taste sensation and culinary diversity, its need, as the saying goes, is a definite must.

SOFT MERINGUE that is spooned onto the plate and then burnt with a kitchen blowtorch is a great alternative to baked meringue. The missing crunch can be added to the dish in other ways such as this vanilla-scented oat crumble. If you don't have a kitchen blowtorch use a hot grill instead but you will need to let the plate cool before finishing the dish.

TAMARILLO & KIWIFRUIT SALAD WITH BURNT MERINGUE, OAT CRUMBLE, LIME & GIN SYRUP

Oat Crumble

2 lrg free-range eggs
1 tsp vanilla extract
1 cup caster sugar
1 tbsp butter, melted & cooled
½ tsp salt
2 tsp baking powder
2 ½ cups finely cut rolled oats

Lime & Gin Syrup

1 lime, the zest finely grated
6 limes, juiced
100 g caster sugar
2 tbsp gin

Tamarillo & Kiwifruit Salad with Burnt Meringue

2 tamarillos
2 kiwifruit, peeled & cross-section sliced
3 free-range egg whites
190 g caster sugar
½ tsp salt

SERVES 4

OAT CRUMBLE

Preheat oven to 180 °C and line two large baking trays with baking paper. Cream the eggs, vanilla and sugar until white and frothy. Stir through the remaining ingredients until well combined. Divide the mixture between the two trays and spread as thinly as possible. Bake for 12 to 15 minutes and then slide the baking paper off the tray onto cooling racks. When cool, crumble the oat mixture and store in an airtight container.

LIME & GIN SYRUP

Heat the lime zest, juice and sugar in a small saucepan until the sugar has dissolved. Remove from the heat and stir through the gin. Leave to cool.

TAMARILLO & KIWIFRUIT SALAD WITH BURNT MERINGUE

Bring a saucepan of water to the boil. Remove the stem and score a cross into the base of the tamarillos before blanching for 30 seconds. Place in a bowl of ice water and then peel the skin away using a paring knife. Slice the tamarillos and arrange on each plate together with the sliced kiwifruit.

Put the egg whites, sugar and salt in a bowl large enough to fit on top of a saucepan of simmering water. Whisk over the simmering water until the egg white mixture reaches 60 °C. Remove from the heat and continue to whisk with an electric mixer for 8 to 10 minutes until the meringue is thick, glossy and cool.

RECIPE CONTINUES >

Place a spoonful of soft meringue next to the slices of kiwifruit and tamarillo and spread into a curved shape using the back of the spoon. Brown the top of the meringue with a blowtorch until evenly coloured.

Pour a little syrup over the fruit and scatter over a little oat crumble before serving.

THE VERY grown-up tastes in this unusual combination of flavours beg to be served with an aromatic tea such as jasmine or soursop. Alternatively, the smoky lapsong souchong would also work very well as an accompanying afternoon tea beverage.

GINGERBREAD WITH PRUNE BUTTER, TAMARILLOS & ORANGE BLOSSOM MASCARPONE

Prune Butter

500 g pitted prunes
250 ml orange juice
1 orange, the zest finely grated
¼ tsp salt
⅓ cup soft brown sugar

MAKES 3 CUPS

Gingerbread

125 g butter
1 cup molasses
1 ½ cups plain flour
½ cup self-raising flour
1 tsp bicarbonate of soda
2 tsp ground ginger
2 tsp ground cinnamon
½ tsp mixed spice
¼ tsp salt
1 cup caster sugar
1 cup milk
2 free-range eggs, lightly beaten

MAKES 2 SML LOAVES

Orange Blossom Mascarpone

250 g mascarpone
2 tsp orange blossom water
2 tbsp icing sugar

PRUNE BUTTER

Combine all of the ingredients in a saucepan except for the brown sugar. Stir and bring to a gentle simmer and cook with the lid on for 20 minutes, stirring every few minutes. Remove the lid and continue to simmer and stir for 3 to 5 minutes until approximately 3 tbsp of liquid remains. Stir in the brown sugar and when dissolved, puree with a stick blender to a coarse consistency.

GINGERBREAD

Preheat oven to 170 °C and grease and line two 23.5 cm x 7.5 cm bar cake pans with baking paper. Warm butter and molasses together in a small saucepan over low heat. Sift the flours, bicarbonate of soda, spices and salt into a medium-sized bowl. Stir through the caster sugar. Make a well and beat the eggs and milk together in it before incorporating the flour mixture to make a smooth batter. Fold the butter and molasses into the batter and divide into the cake pans. Smooth the top before baking in the oven for 40 to 45 minutes. Leave to stand in the tin for 15 minutes, then turn out and leave to cool completely.

ORANGE BLOSSOM MASCARPONE

Mix all the ingredients together until smooth. RECIPE CONTINUES >

TO SERVE

Allowing one half tamarillo per person, bring a saucepan of water to the boil. Remove the stem and score a cross into the base of the tamarillo before blanching for 30 seconds. Place in a bowl of ice water and then peel the skin away using a paring knife.

Slice the gingerbread into pieces 1 cm thick and thickly spread with the Prune Butter and Orange Blossom Mascarpone. Thinly slice the tamarillo and place on top of the mascarpone.

LAMB

JIM WALKER

Lamb or sheep meat has been a minimal part of livestock production in the Southern Forests region; however, Jim Walker's family have raised black-faced Suffolk sheep in the Manjimup area since the late 1960s. This renowned high-quality meat breed has a connection with Jim's English family heritage, and has provided undoubtable pleasure on the plate for some time.

Jim's grandfather came from Durham in the north-east of England in the early 1900s. Bound for the eastern states, but racked with seasickness, he got off the boat in Fremantle. After a short time in Western Australia, he made his way across to Newcastle in New South Wales but returned with a new wife to settle just out of Manjimup in Jardee. Here Jim's father and two siblings were raised, later buying the property nearby on Seven Day Road where Jim and his wife Steff and three young children now live and farm.

Initially starting with dairy and then growing fruit for the cannery that operated in Manjimup in the late 1960s, Jim's family raised sheep for fine wool production during the 1980s when the wool price was at its highest. The price rapidly dropped during the 1990s and as a consequence the Walker's de-stocked their merinos but kept a small amount of black-faced Suffolks. Over the past 20 years, Jim and Steff have further diversified into beef cattle, apples, avocados, truffles and figs.

Three years ago they had the opportunity to buy a small stud flock of black-faced Suffolks, building their numbers further, taking their total amount to 150 head. 'It will remain a sideline for us, keeping things small and manageable from a growing, processing and selling point of view,' Steff explains. 'Despite their high 'cute-ability' they get to their target weight quicker than other breeds, so they're big, very strong, naughty and stubborn, so we keep handling to a minimum and as quiet and as calm as possible.'

Now registered as Manjimup Suffolk, Jim and Steff process small numbers through the Dardanup Butchering Company, which are then butchered, packed and made into sausages by Fox Brothers Butchers in Pemberton. 'We would never receive the premium this beautiful meat deserves through the normal market chain, and we enjoy the direct contact with customers at the Manjimup Farmers Market and at Fonty's Pool,' Jim explains.

In addition, they've had interest from Chinese buyers wishing to purchase registered ewes and rams for their own production, presenting further opportunities and a crossroad for Jim and Steff and their small stud flock. However small or big a producer they choose to become, this highly prized lamb breed is a delicious asset to the diversity of food grown in this area.

AS WITH pork neck, lamb neck is a really underrated cut that has so much flavour and tenderness when cooked long and slow. Aside from being served as an accompaniment to braises, chickpea panisses can also be a delicious snack with drinks when served hot and crispy straight from the pan.

BRAISED LAMB NECK WITH ARTICHOKES, MINT & CHICKPEA PANISSES

Braised Lamb

3 x 450 g whole lamb necks
1 cup plain flour or chickpea flour
salt flakes & freshly
cracked black pepper
30 g unsalted butter
1 onion, roughly chopped
2 sticks celery, roughly chopped
1 carrot, peeled & roughly chopped
2 bay leaves
8 – 10 sprigs fresh thyme
1 cup white wine
1 – 1 ½ litres chicken
or vegetable stock

Chickpea Panisses

1 litre water
1 tbsp olive oil
1 ½ tsp salt
285 g chickpea flour
olive oil, for frying

To Assemble

6 sml – med globe artichokes
salt
2 cups peas, podded
½ cup fresh mint leaves
salt flakes & freshly
cracked black pepper

SERVES 4

BRAISED LAMB

To cook the lamb, preheat oven to 160 °C. Trim the lamb necks of any excess fat. Toss the flour with a little seasoning and dust the lamb necks. Using a large, heavy-based, lidded cast-iron pot, gently brown the lamb necks in the butter. Reserve to the side. Add the vegetables, herbs and wine and stir and simmer for a couple of minutes before returning the lamb necks to the pot. Pour in enough stock to cover. Place a piece of baking paper on the surface and then the lid. Bring to a gentle simmer before transferring to the oven and cooking for 2 ½ to 3 hours until the meat is tender and falls off the bone. Pour the cooking juices from the meat and refrigerate in a wide-mouthed bowl to allow the fat to set on the surface.

CHICKPEA PANISSES

To make the panisses, line a 23 cm square cake tin with baking paper. Heat the water with the oil and salt in a large saucepan. Just before the water simmers, slowly pour in the chickpea flour while whisking. Continue to whisk until the mixture starts to thicken and then stir using a wooden spoon. Place the pot on a simmer mat and cook and stir for 10 minutes until the mixture is very thick. Scrape into the lined baking tin. Using wet hands, pat the surface until even and smooth. Cover with a piece of plastic wrap and then leave to cool before refrigerating.

RECIPE CONTINUES >

TO ASSEMBLE

To complete the dish, lift the fat from the surface of the cooking juices and discard. Strain through a fine sieve and reduce until a little syrupy. Gently take the meat off the lamb neck bones and place in a pre-warmed ovenproof serving dish. Pour the reduced stock over the lamb, cover with aluminium foil and transfer to a 120 °C preheated oven.

Boil the artichokes in a large pot of salted water for 10 to 15 minutes until just tender when the base is pierced with the tip of a paring knife. Drain well before cutting in halves lengthwise and transferring to the lamb dish. Re-cover with the foil and return to the oven to keep warm.

Cut the panisses into eight thick finger-sized pieces and fry in olive oil until golden and crispy. Blanch the peas in salted water and serve together with the panisses, lamb and artichokes. Garnish with fresh mint leaves, salt flakes and freshly cracked black pepper.

CRUMBED AND fried food must be served hot and also benefits greatly when balanced with bitter and hot flavours such as the cardoons and mustard leaves in this recipe. Combine all three before dipping and eating, but if you can't source the cardoons and mustard leaves substitute with witlof or radicchio leaves.

CRUMBED BREAST OF LAMB WITH CARDOONS, MUSTARD GREENS & ANCHOVY MAYONNAISE

Lamb Breast

1 lamb breast (flap)
sea salt & freshly cracked black pepper
1 onion, roughly chopped
1 carrot, roughly chopped
2 sticks celery, roughly chopped
2 fresh bay leaves
6 – 8 sprigs fresh thyme
1 cup white wine

Braised Cardoons

4 young cardoon stalks
2 shallots, sliced thin
1 cup of lamb, beef or vegetable stock, hot
sea salt flakes & freshly cracked black pepper

Anchovy Mayonnaise

6 anchovies, finely chopped
1 garlic clove, crushed
1 lemon, finely grated rind & juice of
1 cup mayonnaise

LAMB BREAST

Preheat oven to 150 °C. Season the lamb breast before placing in a deep, heavy roasting dish. Scatter over the onion, carrot, celery and herbs. Pour in the wine and enough water to cover the surface of the lamb and vegetables. Place a piece of baking paper on top and then a double layer of foil to seal before baking in the oven for 3 hours until the lamb is tender and soft. Leave to cool. Gently slide the lamb rib bones and tough tendon that runs diagonally across the breast out of the meat. Wrap the meat in plastic to seal and refrigerate for a minimum of 2 hours.

BRAISED CARDOONS

Preheat oven to 180 °C. To prepare the cardoons, cut away any leaves on the edges of the stalks. Using a vegetable peeler, remove the stringy fibres from the exterior of the cardoon stalks. Cut the stalks into 5 cm lengths and blanch in boiling salted water. Drain well before placing in a small deep baking dish together with the shallots. Pour over the stock, season and cover with either aluminium foil or a lid. Bake for 20 to 30 minutes until the cardoons are tender. Remove with a slotted spoon and leave to cool.

ANCHOVY MAYONNAISE

To prepare the anchovy mayonnaise, stir the anchovies, garlic, lemon zest and juice through the mayonnaise to combine. Season to taste and spoon into a serving dish. RECIPE CONTINUES >

To Assemble

2 free-range eggs, beaten
1 tbsp milk
3 cups fresh sourdough breadcrumbs
vegetable oil, for frying
salt flakes & freshly
cracked black pepper
1 handful young mustard leaves

SERVES 8 AS A SNACK

TO ASSEMBLE

Beat the eggs and milk together in a medium-sized bowl and place the sourdough crumbs in another bowl. Slice the cold lamb breast into finger-sized pieces before dipping in the egg mixture and coating in the breadcrumbs. Fry in the vegetable oil until golden and crispy. Drain on paper towels before seasoning and serving together with the cardoons and mustard leaves

LAMB SHANKS are no longer the cheapest cut, although in this flavoursome dish they're worth every penny. The celeriac puree is thickened with rice rather than potato, which adds a lovely sweet creamy flavour without detracting from this delicious root vegetable that accompanies lamb so beautifully.

LAMB SHANKS WITH CUMIN, SHERRY, MUSCATELS, PINE NUTS & CELERIAC PUREE

8 sml bunches dried muscatels

1 cup Pedro Ximenez sherry

4 lamb shanks

3 tsp ground cumin

salt flakes & freshly cracked pepper

2 tsp cumin seeds

30 g butter

1 leek, roughly chopped

2 sticks celery, roughly chopped

2 bay leaves

1 – 1 ½ litres lamb or beef stock

500 g celeriac, peeled & diced

500 ml milk

¼ cup Arborio rice

1 ½ tsp salt

30 g unsalted butter, chilled

¼ cup pine nuts, toasted

1 tbsp fresh dill sprigs, to garnish

SERVES 4

Soak the muscatels in the sherry overnight. Preheat oven to 160 °C. Evenly rub the lamb shanks with the ground cumin, salt flakes and pepper. Fry the cumin seeds in the butter in a heavy-based, lidded, cast-iron pot large enough to fit all four shanks, until fragrant. Brown each shank evenly in the cumin seeds and butter and reserve to the side. Gently fry the leek and celery until just starting to soften, and then place the bay leaves and shanks back in the pot. Pour over enough stock to just cover the meat. Place a piece of baking paper directly on the surface and then cover with the lid. Transfer to the oven and cook for 2 ½ to 3 hours until the shanks are tender.

Simmer the celeriac in the milk with the rice and salt for 20 to 30 minutes until the celeriac and rice are very soft. Puree and check the seasoning. Adjust with a little extra milk if needed to make a creamy puree. Reserve in a warm place.

Heat the muscatels and sherry in a microwave or simmer in a saucepan until the muscatels are hot and soft.

Strain the cooking juices from the lamb through a fine sieve and simmer until half the volume. Add 3 tbsp of the sherry from the muscatels and continue to simmer until the sauce becomes syrupy. Whisk in the cold butter until melted and the sauce is velvety and shiny.

Serve the lamb shanks on a bed of celeriac puree garnished with the muscatels, sherry sauce, pine nuts and fresh dill.

LIMES

BRIAN & VAL THORNLEY

Brian Thornley is no stranger to the challenges and rewards of primary production. He has provided more than 30 years of accountancy and management services to small family farms and large corporate groups within and outside the Southern Forests region, so his decision to grow limes was well-informed and greatly aided by valuable local advice.

Together with his wife, Val, Brian purchased a karri-forest flanked property south of Pemberton ten years ago, planting 1,120 Tahitian lime trees in 2010 on five north-to-south undulating, renovated acres with access to abundant high-quality water.

Being very wary of Managed Investment Schemes in agriculture, Brian and Val chose limes for their niche market positioning and potential in an increasingly food-educated market. The fruit's relative easiness to grow, harvest and transport also appealed, making the financial and personal decision-making process a very informed and considered treechange choice.

As well as noting the importance of diverse skill-based team work, one of Brian's observations of today's successful primary production is the need for growers to brand and market their products – either as a collective or individually. 'The input costs of farming have increased dramatically over the years; however, the value of products have not. Getting the marketing mix right is crucial to success.'

Having managed her own media and public relations firm and having been involved with both business and events management for many years, Val also brings valuable experience and knowledge to the task of selling their limes.

Brian estimates that by 2016 they will reach their maximum target of a 50-tonne harvest, which they will endeavour to sell to their current local, high-end retail and restaurant customers, but also into the valuable and rapidly developing Singapore and Kuala Lumpar markets.

Aside from the limes, choosing and developing their utopian patch in Pemberton was also about enjoying their retiring years in the countryside they both greatly enjoy. With onsite operations manager Peter Willis undertaking the day-to-day tasks, Brian and Val are able to take time to enjoy the beautiful view over their property, assured they've made good decisions thanks to the knowledge accrued from many valuable years of observation and planning.

BOUGATSA IS a Greek breakfast pastry that can be served with either a sweet or savoury filling and was the inspiration for this recipe. When served as a sweet pastry it resembles a slightly flatter vanilla slice, although when made with coconut cream and lime it is a much more aromatic version.

GREEK LIME & COCONUT CUSTARD TART

500 ml full cream milk

500 ml coconut cream

2 limes, the peels of removed with a vegetable peeler

3 free-range eggs

5 tbsp corn flour

220 g caster sugar

2 limes, the finely grated zest of

6 tbsp shredded coconut

1 x 375 g pack filo pastry

150 g unsalted butter, melted

½ tsp ground cinnamon

¼ cup caster sugar

icing sugar for dusting

SERVES 12

Heat the milk and coconut cream with the lime peel in a heavy-based saucepan until just simmering. Take off the heat and leave to infuse for 15 minutes before straining into a jug and reserving to the side.

Beat the eggs, cornflour and sugar until fluffy. Gently beat in the lime-infused milk and return to the heavy-based saucepan. Bring to a gentle heat and stir continuously until it thickens. Let it simmer slowly on a simmer mat for 2 minutes and then remove from the heat. Add the shredded coconut and lime zest and transfer to a bowl. Place a piece of baking paper directly onto the surface of the custard and refrigerate until cold.

Preheat the oven to 200 °C. Line a 27 cm x 37 cm lamington baking tin with baking paper. Using three-quarters of the filo pastry sheets, overlap the sheets of pastry over the base and over the sides and top edge of the tin, brushing melted butter in between each layer of pastry. Pour the custard into the tin and then fold the overlapping sides on top. They will not completely cover the surface of the custard. Continue to layer the remaining pastry sheets with the melted butter on top of the custard to create a neat pastry 'lid.' Reserve two final sheets of pastry and place on the top in a ruffled pattern. Brush with a final layer of melted butter before baking 30 to 40 minutes until golden brown and crispy.

Combine the ground cinnamon and remaining caster sugar and evenly sprinkle over the tart before dusting with icing sugar and serving.

MARINE FISH

JUDY DITTMER

A whole book could be written about Judy Dittmer's extraordinary life, but a very abbreviated version of her story starts with her being born into fishing. Her father, George, was one of the early pioneers of the south-coast salmon fishing industry in the mid 1940s. Her childhood was spent travelling from one lighthouse to another along the West Australian coast. She later trained as a nurse at Royal Perth Hospital, in the early 1960s.

Following her parents back to Augusta, Judy enjoyed the challenges and diversity of country nursing. She also worked in an operating theatre, and seeking more experience in this area, Judy trained at the Royal Women's Hospital in Brisbane, after which she worked in a private hospital.

Always keen for an adventure, Judy went to nurse wounded local civilians in Vietnam in 1971 under the SEATO (South East Asian Treaty Organization), which profoundly changed her life, as did the difficult return and transition back home.

On returning to Australia, Judy joined her mother at Windy Harbour to take on commercial fishing, an extraordinarily physically demanding job in often treacherous conditions, and in one of the most isolated spots in Western Australia. She also provided her very experienced nursing services at the Northcliffe Nursing Post.

As one of only three resident Wetline Commercial Fishers, Judy's services to nursing and fishing in the Windy Harbour and Northcliffe communities share the same quiet pioneering spirit (and she has the same wonderful dry sense of humour) this region was founded on.

JIM ROBB

Jim and Judy are second cousins; however, Jim's early start was in the Collie coalmines as a diesel fitter. He started commercial gill and long-line fishing in Busselton in the 1980s and then moved further south to Augusta and Windy Harbour, harvesting rock lobster and mostly shark fishing.

He is now one of five operating shark fishers in the south-west, although Jim also catches other species including pink snapper, groper, queen snapper and dhufish. Jim fishes with a crew of two others out of Windy Harbour, except for during the extreme winter months of June and July.

Fish are cleaned at sea, and brought into shore to be packed in layers of ice before being driven to Busselton or Manjimup where they are then couriered to Perth for filleting, packing and then selling into the local market.

With a size limit that equates to approximately 18 kg in weight, sharks are fished predominantly for the takeaway fish and chip market, although competition with cheaper but inferior frozen imported product has put increasing cost pressures on this sector in the industry.

Now of retirement age, Jim says he's happy to keep fishing for as long as his good health continues and demand for fresh local fish remains.

One of the most popular recreational fishing opportunities in the year at Windy Harbour is around Easter time when the Australian salmon are in abundance along the south coast of Western Australia. However, throughout the rest of the year, many other saltwater fish species can be found in the waters off Windy Harbour.

The south coast region's diversity is affected by the warm tropical Leeuwin Current that together with the southerly cold-water provide a diversity of species, including the superb West Australian dhufish, nannygai, pink snapper, hapuka and King George whiting.

Professional fisherman and licensed abalone divers have reduced in numbers over the years at Windy Harbour as a result of limited access, difficult weather conditions associated with isolated, unprotected waters, and rising costs. However, recreational fishing opportunities are still greatly enjoyed by the locals.

Check the Department of Fisheries Western Australia website for detailed information on species identification, and number and size limits.

MARJORAM AND borage are herbs that have a wonderful affinity with fish. In this dish their flavour is as important as their beautiful appearance as a garnish.

SNAPPER WITH TOASTED QUINOA, MARJORAM, BORAGE & BUTTERED SORREL

1 cup red quinoa

2 cups water

1 tsp salt

1 med shallot, finely chopped

¼ cup dry white wine

¼ cup apple cider vinegar

250 g unsalted cultured butter

salt flakes & freshly cracked
black pepper

4 x 180 – 200 g thick snapper fillets

30 g unsalted butter

sea salt flakes &
freshly cracked black pepper

1 sml handful sorrel leaves, ribs
removed & leaves torn

1 tbsp marjoram leaves & flowers

8 – 10 borage flowers

SERVES 4

Simmer the quinoa in the water with the salt for 20 minutes until tender. Drain well and spread out thinly on a baking tray. Toast in a preheated 180 °C oven for 30 to 40 minutes until toasted and crunchy.

Cook the shallot in the wine and vinegar until nearly three-quarters reduced. Strain through a fine sieve, pressing to extract as much of the wine and vinegar reduction as possible. Return the reduction to the saucepan and discard the shallot. On a low heat, whisk the 250 g cultured butter into the reduction until creamy and emulsified. Season to taste and reserve in a warm place.

Season before panfrying the snapper fillets in the 30 g butter for 3 to 4 minutes per side depending on the thickness of the fish.

Divide the sorrel evenly on the plates and pour over a little of the butter sauce. Place the snapper on top and then spoon a little of the toasted quinoa on top of each of the snapper fillets. Garnish with the marjoram leaves and flowers and borage flowers.

ADMITTEDLY, FRESH abalone is not the easiest nor cheapest ingredient to source; however, it's worth seeking out when in season to prepare this delicious dish. An alternative is to use thinly sliced squid or baby octopus.

STIR-FRIED ABALONE WITH CUCUMBER, HORSERADISH CREAM & DILL OIL

15 g (+ ½ cup) fresh dill

100 ml extra virgin olive oil

2 tbsp fresh horseradish, finely grated

1 cup crème fraîche or sour cream

½ tsp caster sugar

salt flakes & freshly
cracked black pepper

2 whole brownlip or greenlip
abalone, freshly shucked, cleaned,
scrubbed & trimmed

2 tbsp grapeseed oil

3 sml Lebanese cucumbers, peeled,
deseeded & cut into 1 cm thick pieces

1 tbsp lemon juice

4 lemon wedges

SERVES 4 AS A STARTER

Completely emulsify the 15 g dill with extra virgin olive oil in a blender. Fold the grated horseradish through the crème fraîche together with the caster sugar and season to taste.

Using a very sharp knife, slice the abalone as thinly as possible. Heat a heavy-based frying pan or wok until smoking hot and pour in 1 tbsp grapeseed oil. Gently throw half the sliced abalone into the pan or wok and stirfry for 2 minutes. Reserve to the side and repeat with the second batch of abalone. Heat the pan again, stirfry the cucumber for 2 to 3 minutes and add the abalone, tossing with the lemon juice, some salt flakes and freshly cracked black pepper. Spoon onto the plates and drizzle over a little dill oil. Serve with a dollop of horseradish cream and garnish with the remaining fresh dill and lemon wedges.

MARRON

SUE & RAY HARRIS

'It was a little boy's turned old fella's dream,' says Sue as she talks pragmatically about her and her husband Ray's last 10 years establishing the region's second largest marron growing facility in Northcliffe. 'You forget how far you've come until someone asks you to tell them your story.'

With a background in building development and nursing management, Ray and Sue had a working lifetime of Perth-based planning, financial management and problem solving behind them before moving onto their 147-acre property in 2003.

Of retirement age but with determined goals in place, they planned a four-stage process of creating a sustainable, self-funded farming business with a lifestyle that allowed them time off during the year. It is close to being realised, with a projected 3 tonne harvest of premium grade marron in 2014.

Marron are the largest freshwater crayfish in Western Australia and the third largest in the world. Endemic to the south-west, marron are river recyclers that play a critical role in breaking down animal and plant matter that sink to the bottom. They do not tolerate high salinity, low oxygen or high temperatures, and, unlike other freshwater crayfishes such as koonacs and gilgies, marron only live in permanent water bodies such as larger rivers and dams.

'Like horses, they all have a birthday once a year at Christmas time,' Sue explains. The season for marron growers supplying from purpose built drain-down ponds (as opposed to permanent farm dams) is from April to September. Marron take 2 ½ years to grow from a juvenile to saleable size, and Sue and Ray manage four growth processes across their 39 ponds at any one time.

Selective breeding for the highest quality provides them with a premium product which they sell to the three main distributors in Western Australia: Forest Fresh Marron in Pemberton, Blue Ridge Marron in Manjimup and WA Marron in Donnybrook.

Uniquely, marron that are strong, clean, chilled and in good condition can survive 7 to 10 days out of the water when carefully transported in styrofoam boxes with ice packs and damp foam. Aside from their delicious sweet flavour, which is highly prized, high-end restaurants around the world also appreciate this transport system, which allows supply without compromising quality due to distance and transport times.

Sue and Ray see further potential for their property in the future; but in the meantime, and with good health prevailing in their later years, their focus remains on producing a luxury quality product that is a historical and highly valued regional culinary signature for the Southern Forests.

THIS DISH is in the classic Danish tradition of open sandwiches, which they call Smørrebrød. The toppings can be varied infinitely but a slice of rye bread is always the base upon which they're made. The recipe here for black bread is even more complex in flavour than straight rye bread, but an equally superb base for this quick carrot, dill and caraway pickle that tastes delicious with the marron.

MARRON, BLACK BREAD, CARROT, DILL & CARAWAY PICKLE WITH SOUR CREAM

Marron

4 x 250 – 300 g live marron
¼ cup salt
1 loaf black bread, sliced
2 cups carrot, dill & caraway pickle
1 cup sour cream
sea salt & freshly
cracked black pepper

SERVES 4

Carrot, Dill & Caraway Pickle

1 litre apple cider vinegar
220 g white sugar
1 tbsp sea salt flakes
1 tbsp caraway seeds
2 fresh bay leaves
800 g carrot, coarsely grated
100 g currants
¼ cup fresh dill

SERVES 8

MARRON

Place the live marron in the freezer for 20 to 30 minutes until the marron no longer moves but is not yet frozen. Bring a large stockpot of water to the boil and add the salt. Gently put the marron in the boiling water, cover immediately and cook for 7 to 8 minutes. Remove from the pot and plunge into iced water. Twist and pull the head away from the tail. Using kitchen scissors cut up the middle of the inside of the tail and ease the flesh away from the shell. Pull back the flap from the top of the meat and gently remove the alimentary canal. Slice the marron meat in halves.

CARROT, DILL & CARAWAY PICKLE

Bring the cider vinegar, sugar, salt, caraway seeds and bay leaves to a simmer, stirring to dissolve the sugar and salt. Place the carrot and currants in a medium-sized bowl and pour over the hot pickling syrup. Level the top of the carrot with the back of a spoon, ensuring it is below the surface of the syrup. Lay a piece of plastic wrap directly on the surface and refrigerate overnight. When ready to serve, drain the carrot and stir through the fresh dill. RECIPE CONTINUES >

Black Bread

2 ¼ tsp dry yeast

350 ml warm water

1 tsp soft brown sugar

2 tbsp cocoa powder

2 tbsp coffee, espresso ground

¼ cup molasses

3 tsp caraway seeds

60 g unsalted butter, diced

2 tsp salt

150 g rye flour

425 g (+ extra) strong plain flour

150 g potato, peeled &
coarsely grated

3 tbsp vegetable oil

2 tbsp milk

**MAKES 2 SML LOAVES OR
2 LRG BAGUETTES**

BLACK BREAD

Dissolve the yeast in half of the water together with the brown sugar. Leave 5 minutes until frothy. Combine the cocoa, coffee, molasses, caraway seeds, butter and salt in a small saucepan and stir while gently warming to dissolve. Place the rye and plain flour in a large bowl and mix through the grated potato. Make a well and pour in the molasses mixture, the remaining warm water and yeast mixture. Using a large spoon, mix to bring together a soft dough. Turn the dough out onto a floured work surface and knead for 5 minutes. Pour the vegetable oil into the dough bowl and return the dough to the bowl, rolling it around in the oil to coat. Cover with plastic wrap and allow to rise by half its size again. Tip the dough back onto the work surface, divide in halves and shape into either baguettes or small loaves. Place onto a baking paper–lined baking tray and leave until it's risen by half its size again. Preheat oven to 220 °C. Brush the loaves with the milk and bake for 20 minutes. Reduce the heat to 180 °C and bake a further 20 minutes. Cool on a wire rack.

TO SERVE

Make a little pile of marron on the plate and serve with some carrot, dill & caraway pickle, black bread, sour cream, salt flakes and freshly cracked black pepper, for guests to make their own open sandwiches.

THIS DRESSING is a lovely, soft way of including garlic in a salad without it dominating the other more subtle flavours. Nuts and nut oils work wonderfully well with any freshwater shellfish – particularly marron!

MARRON, ROASTED WALNUT, AVOCADO & BARTLETT PEAR SALAD WITH A CANDIED GARLIC VERJUICE DRESSING

1 cup walnuts
6 cloves garlic
extra virgin olive oil
4 x 300 g live marron
¼ cup salt
400 ml verjuice
80 ml walnut oil
2 handfuls salad greens that include bitter varieties
3 stalks celery, thinly sliced (optional)
1 avocado, sliced
2 sml Bartlett pears, thinly sliced
1 sml bunch fresh dill, the tips plucked from the stalks
freshly cracked black pepper

SERVES 4

Dry roast the walnuts in a 200 °C oven for 20 minutes until just brown then transfer to a dry tea towel. Gather the corners of the tea towel together and rub the skins away from the walnuts. Transfer to a coarse sieve to separate the skins from the roasted walnut. Reserve to the side.

Blanch garlic cloves in boiling water before peeling. Using a simmer mat, gently warm the garlic in enough extra virgin olive oil to just cover, until the cloves just start to turn a warm blond colour. Leave to cool before removing the garlic and reserving the olive oil for another dish.

Place the live marron in the freezer for 20 to 30 minutes until the marron no longer moves but is not yet frozen. Bring a large stockpot of water to the boil and add the salt. Gently put the marron in the boiling water, cover immediately and cook for 3 minutes. Remove from the pot and plunge into iced water. Twist and pull the head away from the tail. Using kitchen scissors cut up the middle of the inside of the tail and ease the flesh away from the shell. Pull back the flap from the top of the meat and gently remove the alimentary canal. Slice the marron meat in halves.

In a shallow pan, simmer the verjuice until reduced by half. Add the marron halves to just warm then remove with a slotted spoon reserving to the side. Whisk the garlic cloves and walnut oil into the warm verjuice.

Compile the salad by scattering the salad leaves on a platter, topped with the celery slices, marron halves, sliced avocado and pear. Drizzle over the dressing and garnish with the roasted walnuts, fresh dill tips and freshly cracked black pepper.

MILK & CREAM

MAT & ROBERT DAUBNEY

Enormous hardship and ultimate failure characterised the Group Settlement Scheme. One of the few families that survived – exemplifying the resilience and hard work needed to endure the adversity and, at best primitive, early conditions – was the Daubney family in Northcliffe.

Group 121 Northcliffe was where James Robert Daubney arrived from the UK in 1924, purchasing 130 acres of heavily forested land which he cleared in 25-acre lots to establish a dairy farm. His wife Edith (nee Bannister) arrived some 18 months later to a vista very unlike the picture-book pastoral images on the promotional posters.

Having no option to turn back and with some general farming experience that including stock and horse management, which was a significant advantage over many other settlers who had no farming experience, James and Edith developed the land and made a home and life that included eleven children.

All eleven children worked on the property, but two sons Robert and Les, who are now in their so-called retiring years, remain involved in day-to-day farming duties on Group Settlement 121, that is now over 3,000 acres and known as Bannister Downs Farm.

Robert's son Mat and his wife, Sue, have gone on to establish Bannister Downs Farm as one of Western Australia's leading independent single-origin dairies. They practice sustainable farming methods and use modern processing and packaging equipment. They have over 1,500 Holstein Fresian cows to produce vertically integrated, high-quality and award-winning milk, cream and other value-added dairy products.

Mat credits their success to not only the gifted business leadership skills of his wife, Sue, and the physical efforts required of each family member involved, but the family's collective support when making those leap-of-faith decisions necessary to survive. 'Even though they may have thought we were crazy, they didn't say so, choosing instead to support the next generation's efforts to grow the business.'

Despite the common myths and perceptions of primary production being an unsophisticated rural pursuit practised by archetypal wholesome farmers, the Daubney family – who have supported each generation with higher education, innovation and the pursuit of the highest quality possible – demonstrate a modern farming family that is anything but what the mainstream media often portray.

Bannister Downs Farm is a regional and state culinary asset that continues the pioneering legacy James and Edith began 90 years ago. Should they choose to, their great grandchildren have every opportunity to continue and grow this regional icon, with the loyalty of West Australian consumers and supportive government policies necessary to keep our local producers in healthy viable production.

THIS RECIPE was inspired by the very talented chef Luke Burgess. In his original version he used Lapsong Souchong tea to infuse the cream. Here I've used chamomile tea, which creates a soft herbal taste that's inherently comforting, and lovely with tangy rhubarb.

CHAMOMILE CREAM WITH RHUBARB JELLY & GINGER THIN CRUMBS

Chamomile Cream

250 ml full cream milk
250 ml cream
5 g loose dried chamomile tea
pinch salt
50 g caster sugar
2 titanium-strength gelatine leaves

Rhubarb Jelly

500 g rhubarb, roughly chopped
½ cup caster sugar
500 ml water
pinch salt
1 titanium-strength gelatine leaf

To Serve

4 Ginger Thin biscuits, crumbled
icing sugar

SERVES 4

CHAMOMILE CREAM

To make the chamomile cream, heat the milk and cream together until just simmering. Stir through the chamomile tea and allow to steep for a minimum of 2 hours. Strain through a sieve lined with a damp muslin cloth, return to the saucepan and gently reheat together with the salt and sugar, stirring to dissolve. Soak the two titanium gelatine leaves in water for 3 to 4 minutes until softened. Squeeze the excess water from the gelatine leaves and stir through the cream mixture to dissolve. Pour into four 250 ml serving dishes and refrigerate until set.

RHUBARB JELLY

To make the rhubarb jelly, simmer the rhubarb together with the caster sugar, water and salt for 5 to 10 minutes until the rhubarb is a soft pulp. Strain through a sieve lined with a damp muslin cloth and discard the pulp. Gently reheat the 250 ml rhubarb juice in a small saucepan. Soak the titanium gelatine leaf in water for 3 to 4 minutes until softened. Squeeze the excess water from the gelatine leaf and stir through the rhubarb juice to dissolve.

Pour into a jug and refrigerate until cold but still pourable. Evenly pour on the tops of each set chamomile cream. Refrigerate until set.

TO SERVE

Serve with a scattering of crumbled Ginger Thin biscuits on top of the jelly and a little dusting of icing sugar.

TRES LECHES is Spanish for 'three milks' and this recipe is a popular cake throughout the United States, Mexico, Central and South America. A simple sponge or butter cake is soaked in three types of milks; however, here I've chosen to substitute the cream for the slightly lighter crème fraîche.

LATIN AMERICAN TRES LECHES CAKE WITH STRAWBERRY & ROSE

Tres Leches Cake

300 g plain flour
2 tsp baking powder
6 free-range eggs, separated
pinch salt
275 g caster sugar
½ cup milk
1 tsp vanilla extract
500 ml sweetened condensed milk
400 ml evaporated milk
300 ml crème fraîche

Strawberries & Rose

3 punnets strawberries, washed & tops removed
½ cup caster sugar
2 tsp rose water
½ cup dried rose petals

Meringue Topping

360 g caster sugar
120 ml water
160 g free-range egg white (from approx. 4 lrg eggs)
pinch salt
3 tsp rose water

Tres Leches Sauce

120 ml sweetened condensed milk
90 ml evaporated milk
70 ml crème fraîche

SERVES 15

TRES LECHES CAKE

Preheat oven to 180 °C and line a lamington baking tin with baking paper. Sift the flour, baking powder and salt together and reserve to the side. Whisk the egg whites until frothy and then gradually add the sugar and continue to beat until a firm meringue. Add the yolks one at a time until incorporated and light and frothy. In a separate bowl, combine the milk and vanilla extract. Fold in the flour mixture and vanilla milk alternately until well combined. Spoon into the lamington tin, smooth the top and bake for 25 to 35 minutes until a skewer comes away clean when inserted.

Combine the condensed and evaporated milks and crème fraîche. With the cake still in the tin, evenly pierce holes halfway into the cake with a skewer and pour over this milk mixture. Cover and refrigerate overnight to absorb.

STRAWBERRIES & ROSE

To prepare the strawberries, preheat oven to 220 °C. Halve the strawberries and evenly scatter on a baking tray. Sprinkle over the caster sugar and bake in the oven for 10 minutes until the strawberries have collapsed a little and the sugar has dissolved into the strawberry juices. Allow to cool before transferring into a bowl. Stir through the rose water, cover and refrigerate.

RECIPE CONTINUES >

MERINGUE TOPPING

To make the meringue topping, combine the caster sugar and water in a small saucepan. Bring to a simmer and stir to dissolve. Continue to cook until the syrup reaches 120 °C on a sugar thermometer. Meanwhile, whisk the egg whites with a pinch of salt until they form soft peaks. Gradually pour in the hot syrup while continuing to whisk until the meringue is thick and glossy. Whisk in the rose water. Spoon onto the cake in an even layer.

TRES LECHES SAUCE

For the three milks sauce, combine the evaporated and condensed milks and crème fraîche. Serve a square piece of cake in a bowl and then pour a little of the three milks sauce around the base of the cake. Spoon some of the strawberries onto the sauce with a sprinkling of dried rose petals over the top to garnish.

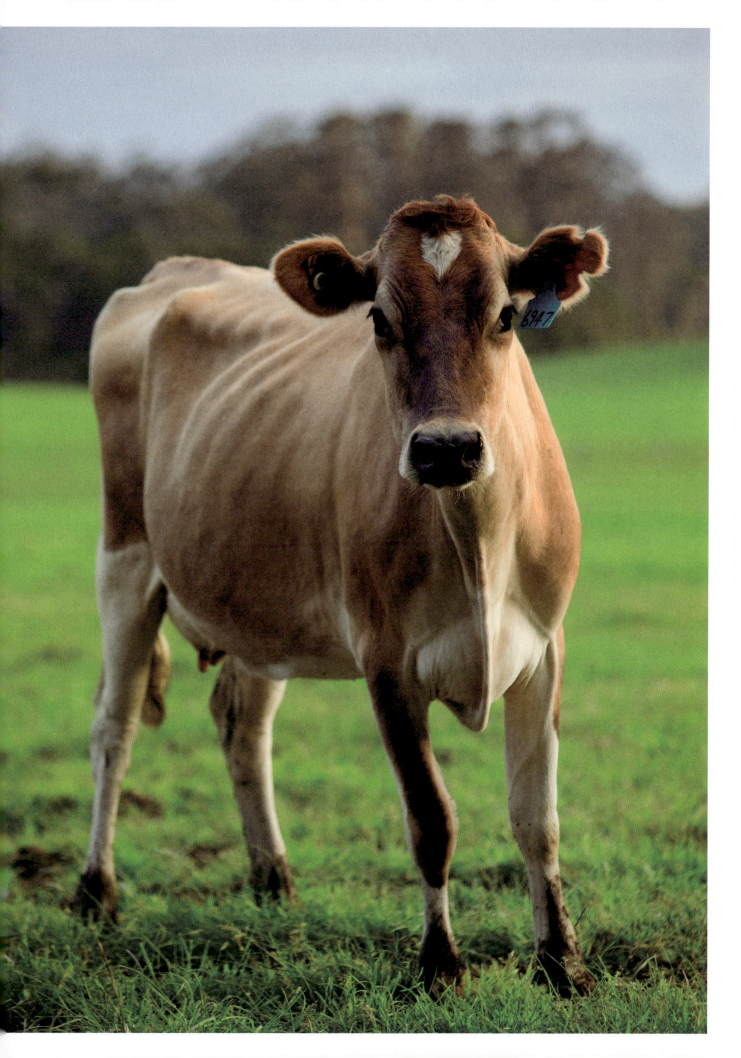

BUTTER MADE from the cream produced by cows who feed on mixed green pastures has a delicious almost herbaceous flavour that couldn't be a more direct paddock-to-plate taste experience.

FRESHLY CHURNED BUTTER

2 x 600 ml pouches Bannister Downs whipping cream
2 tsp salt flakes

MAKES APPROXIMATELY 500 G

Whip the cream in the bowl of an electric mixer on medium speed for 15 to 20 minutes until the butter has formed into a lump around the whisk and the buttermilk has pooled at the bottom of the bowl.

Strain off the buttermilk, which can be used for other recipes such as pancakes.

Rinse the butter under cold water until the water runs clear. The cleaner the butter, the longer the shelf life. Using your hands, squeeze as much of the water out of the butter as possible. Return to a clean dry bowl of an electric mixer and beat in the salt flakes.

Using aluminium foil, roll into two 250 g logs or press into a container or mould of your choice.

OLIVE OIL

LUIGI BAZZANI

Luigi (Lui) Bazzani arrived relatively late in the history of Italians migrating to Manjimup; however, his working life in Australia had already long been established elsewhere.

Arriving in Melbourne from Lucca, Tuscany in 1952 as a young 19-year-old man, Lui travelled across to Perth via a farm in Cooke Plains in South Australia. He settled in Perth in 1953, working in various labouring jobs, including the Armadale Brickworks, to be able to establish his own property and plant nursery in Cannington.

With horticulture experience accrued from his father in Tuscany, Lui and his wife Angelina (Lina) started Olea Nurseries in 1960. Throughout the mid-1960s, Australia's first olive boom created a strong demand, so along with roses, which Lui also specialised in, Olea developed as a large wholesale nursery supplying olive, pome and various stone-fruit trees.

In a short time, Lui and Lina wished to further expand Olea Nurseries. Being in search of better quality soils and water, and having worked with a member of the Pesotto family from Manjimup at the Armadale Brickworks, they came to visit, and eventually purchased a 326-acre property in West Manjimup in 1966.

Initially they grew potatoes and beef cattle while developing the nursery. Along with a vegetable patch for their own use, Lui and Lina planted several Leccino, New Norcia Mission and Frantoio varieties of olives shortly after their arrival. Over the past 20 years they have pressed their own oil, enjoying it over the year in various ways that include the traditional Tuscan vegetable and dried bean dishes.

Rootstocks for tree nurseries take years to develop and build stock levels. With time and dedication, the Bazzani family has placed Olea Nurseries as one of the largest wholesale pome, stone and olive tree suppliers in Australia: 30% of their stock goes to retail nurseries, 70% to commercial fruit growers and half of all their production into the eastern states.

As they're now in retirement at 82 years old, Lui and Lina's son David together with his wife, Leanne, manage the Manjimup and Donnybrook operations of Olea Nurseries, which specialise in stone and pome fruits. Their daughter Linda handles the olives and roses at their Waroona nursery, which now trades as Mission Horticulture. Their other daughter Lea has followed on from her parents' love of good food and is now the head chef at the nearby Wine & Truffle Company.

On the morning I spoke with Lina, Lui had just walked in with a handful of freshly picked zucchinis from his beloved vegetable garden. 'I can't cook but I boy can I eat!' Lui chuckled. 'Today we'll be having radicchio for lunch, but on Fridays when I help Lea, I'll cook Lui the white beans or borlotti beans with our olive oil which he loves and eats with either tuna or anchovies,' Lina explains.

It's easy to forget the nurseryman behind the growers as equal pioneers. In regard to the olive, olive oil and various fruit-growing industries in Australia, Luigi Bazzani and Olea Nurseries have been major contributors of whom the Southern Forests can be proud.

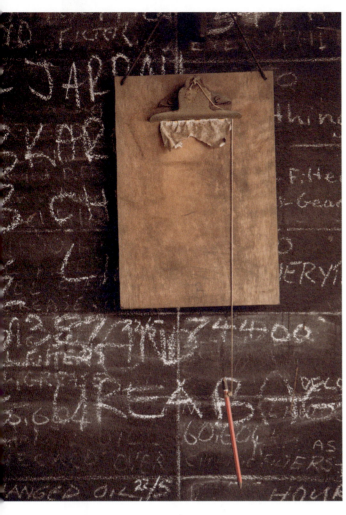

MACEDONIAN MIGRANTS have grown Manjimup white beans for many years, however, cannellini beans are very similar and found in most supermarkets. White beans have been important to the Tuscans in Italy, who braise them slowly in fruity fresh extra virgin olive oil. This delicious version of beans on toast draws on this traditional recipe but serves it in a more familiar style.

EXTRA VIRGIN OLIVE OIL & SUMMER SAVOURY–BRAISED MANJIMUP WHITE BEANS ON TOAST

500 g dried Manjimup white beans or cannellini beans

1 tbsp salt

3 fresh bay leaves

3 garlic cloves

4 sprigs summer savoury or thyme

1 litre extra virgin olive oil

5 thick slices toasted sourdough bread

1 tbsp summer savoury or thyme, roughly chopped

salt flakes & freshly cracked black pepper

SERVES 4

Soak the beans in cold water overnight. Drain, rinse and transfer to a large saucepan. Cover with fresh water and bring to the boil. Simmer for 20 minutes and then add the salt. Continue to simmer another 20 minutes until the beans are just tender. Drain and return to the saucepan. Add the bay leaves, garlic cloves and summer savoury and cover with the extra virgin olive oil. Transfer the pot to a simmer mat and cook the beans on the lowest heat possible for 2 hours until the beans are creamy and soft.

Tear one of the slices of sourdough bread into small pieces and gently fry in a little of the oil taken from the beans until golden.

Toast the other four slices of bread. Remove the beans from the oil with a slotted spoon and serve on the toast, garnished with the golden crumbs, summer savoury, salt flakes and freshly cracked black pepper.

THE ROSEMARY, lavender and olive oil flavours in this cake transport you to the south of France and the almond meal and semolina give the texture a fine gravelly crumb, which contributes to keeping it fresher for longer – if you can resist not finishing it before.

SEMOLINA & ALMOND OLIVE OIL CAKE WITH ROSEMARY & LAVENDER SUGAR

Semolina & Almond Cake

200 g almonds
200 g semolina
¼ tsp salt
1 tbsp baking powder
3 lrg free-range eggs
2 lemons, finely zested
100 ml lemon juice
1 orange, finely zested & juiced
200 g caster sugar
2 tsp rosemary, finely chopped
200 ml extra virgin olive oil

Rosemary & Lavendar Sugar

2 tbsp culinary dried lavender
2 tbsp rosemary, roughly chopped
½ cup caster sugar

SERVES 8

Preheat oven to 200 °C. Place the almonds on a baking tray and roast for 20 minutes until lightly browned and roasted. Leave to cool before grinding to a fine texture in a food processor. Reduce the temperature of the oven to 160 °C and line a 22 cm spring form baking tin with baking paper.

Combine the prepared almond meal together with the semolina, salt and baking powder.

Using an electric mixer, whisk the eggs, lemon and orange zest together with the 200 g caster sugar until frothy and light. Mix the finely chopped rosemary into the olive oil and with the mixer beating, slowly pour the olive oil mixture and citrus juices into the egg mixture alternately with the dry mixture. Spoon into the prepared baking tin, smoothing the top. Bake in the oven for 40 to 45 minutes, until firm in the middle. Mix the dried lavender and roughly chopped rosemary with the ½ cup caster sugar. Sprinkle generously over the warm cake before serving.

PERSIMMONS

TOM & FAYE BACKHOUSE

From forestry to farming, Tom and Faye Backhouse settled in Pemberton in 1976 after time in Grimwade, Walpole and Quinninup with the Forestry Department. 'Faye was very upset leaving Grimwade, crying all the way to Walpole until we stopped just outside at a lookout. She was much happier after she saw the view as she thought it was like Surfers Paradise,' recalls Tom.

They initially purchased 10 acres against the Warren National Park, south of Pemberton, in 1984 and then a further 5 acres in 1986. Starting out with planting avocados, they decided to also plant fifty persimmon trees in 1992. They now farm on an 88-acre area together with their son Tim.

'My mother loved the astringent type of persimmon and used to leave them until they were very soft and then really tuck in. She introduced Faye to them and she also really liked them, so we planted a couple of those, but the rest were the non-astringent Fuyu and Suruga varieties,' Tom explains.

'In 1994 we planted another 100 trees, but pulled them out a few years later. We received good prices one year, but as we don't use any chemicals we had problems with the calyx splitting, and getting enough sunshine for good colour in our protected location.'

As with tomatoes, grapes and avocados, persimmons are not generally considered a berry but in terms of botanical structure and form are classified as such. When cut in half crossways, the beautiful star-like seed pattern is revealed. Their sweet, faintly apricot and melon taste combines well with the stronger flavours of blue cheese, smoked meats, avocado or bitter greens.

Tom and Faye also delight in the stunningly beautiful sight in autumn as the leaves of their persimmon trees go through the various red and orange colours of the season then fall and leave the bauble-like fruit hanging on naked branches. They now only sell their persimmons into local shops and from their roadside stall, and enjoy them both fresh and dried.

Farming mostly avocados with persimmons, truffles and a small amount of waratah flowers on the side, Tom and Faye will continue to produce quality fruit. They consider their forest-sheltered property close to the coast their piece of paradise.

THIS RECIPE was inspired by Dinah Brocksopp, who is the wife of the legendary West Australian viticulturalist John Brocksopp. Dinah served blue cheese on dried persimmons one evening with their delicious Viognier and it was a heavenly match. The walnut spelt bread simply adds a nutty flavour and the witlof a pleasant bitter crunch. You can successfully freeze the extra walnut spelt bread made in this recipe for another time.

DRIED PERSIMMONS, BLUE CHEESE, WALNUT SPELT BREAD & WITLOF

Walnut Spelt Bread

500 g (+ extra) plain white strong flour
500 g (+ extra) wholemeal spelt flour
20 g salt
1 tbsp dried yeast
600 – 650 ml warm water
300 g walnuts, roughly chopped
vegetable oil

MAKES 8 BAGUETTES

Dried Persimmons

1 kg Fuyu persimmons

To Assemble

200 g creamy blue cheese, crumbled
12 x 1 cm thick slices walnut spelt bread
melted butter
2 red or yellow witlof, leaves separated & bases trimmed
12 slices of dried persimmon

SERVES 4 AS A CANAPÉ, ALLOWING 3 PIECES PER PERSON

WALNUT SPELT BREAD

Put the flours and salt in a large bowl and make a well. Place the yeast in the well, add 100 ml of the warm water and mix with a little of the flours to make a thin slurry. Leave 10 minutes until frothy. Add the remaining water and walnuts and mix together to make a roughly lumpy mixture. Tip onto a clean work surface, scraping the bowl clean, and knead for 10 minutes to make a smooth, tight dough. Use a little extra plain flour if the dough is sticky. Drizzle a little vegetable oil into the bowl and swirl the dough around in the oil to coat. Cover the surface of the dough with plastic wrap and leave an hour or so until it rises by half the volume again.

Divide the dough into eight and roll into baguettes. Place on two baking paper–lined trays and sprinkle with a little spelt flour. Leave covered with a dry tea towel for 30 to 45 minutes. Preheat oven to 220 °C. Bake for 20 minutes and then reduce the temperature to 180 °C and bake a further 20 minutes. Leave to cool on a wire rack.

DRIED PERSIMMONS

Leaving the peel on, crosscut persimmons into 5 mm slices and place on dehydrator racks. Following the manufacturer's instructions, dry the sliced persimmon until a soft leather texture. Store in sealed containers. RECIPE CONTINUES >

TO ASSEMBLE

Brush the slices of walnut spelt bread with the melted butter and bake in a preheated 200 °C oven on baking trays for 15 to 20 minutes until golden and toasted. Allow to cool before spreading a little blue cheese on each, topping with a witlof leaf, dried persimmon slice and extra blue cheese.

PORK

SUSAN & ALLAN RONK

Susan and Allan's 40-hectare property north-east of Pemberton is an oasis in the forest. It was purchased in 1994 with little more than bracken, wild blackberry and a pecan orchard, but with Susan's love of growing things and Allan's knowledge and skill of building it has become a home and a private haven diverse with life and energy.

Together, Susan and Allan divide their time between their geology work on field trips throughout the year, and tending their farm. They have extensive ornamental and kitchen gardens and several much-loved Wessex Saddleback pigs.

Susan has long had a fondness for pigs, the fourth most intelligent creature on earth, and highly sentient. In 2003, Susan and Allan began small-scale farming this special breed with six sows, after being introduced to Fiona Chambers – one of Australia's greatest advocates of conserving this unique breed, who with her husband Nicholas farmed this endangered pig in Daylesford, Victoria.

The Wessex Saddleback pig had been common in the UK for centuries and considered to be the ideal breed for bacon; however, as commercial pig farming practices intensified after the Second World War, this slow-growing breed that is particularly suited for foraging in woodland areas was phased out, resulting in extinction there. Fortunately, pedigreed animals had been imported into Australia prior to its demise.

Originally a cross between an Essex pig and British Saddleback, this lop-eared breed is easily identifiable by its black coat and the white stripe over its shoulders. Knowing that the Wessex Saddleback's great foraging skills contributed to the flavour of the meat, Susan and Allan planted a large orchard of chestnut trees for the pigs to forage and fatten under, and the pigs devour the sweet chestnuts in addition to a special grain mix Susan and Allan developed and mill themselves.

Despite greatly enjoying good relationships with chefs, whom Susan and Allan had directly supplied, the logistics and welfare issues of transporting their beautiful rare-breed animals over long distances to the nearest abattoir facilities, the butchering, packing, and transport costs, together with maintaining continuous supply as a small grower, has made a small-scale commercial enterprise unviable.

For now, this labour of love is for occasional private customers or for hobbyists interested in raising heritage breeds for their own meat – the surest way to protect and conserve rare farming animals.

MYRTLE IS a common ornamental shrub but uncommonly used in cooking except in Sardinia, Italy. It imparts an almost juniper-like flavour to food, but like bay leaf is unpalatable and tough to eat. The myrtle berries are very tannic, but can also be used to impart a resinous flavour. Black vinegar is a Chinese ingredient similar to balsamic but with a smokier flavour. It can be easily found in Asian grocery stores. Along with the coffee and prunes in this dish, these flavouring ingredients provide a deeply rich and deliciously gutsy winter dish.

PORK SHOULDER, DRIED APPLE, PRUNES, COFFEE, MYRTLE & BLACK VINEGAR

Prune Butter

500 g pitted prunes
250 ml orange juice
1 orange, the zest finely grated
¼ tsp salt
⅓ cup soft brown sugar

Dehydrated Apple

1 kg Granny Smith
or Pink Lady apples

Pork Shoulder

1 x 2 ½ kg boned pork shoulder with or without rind attached
salt flakes & freshly cracked black pepper
2 cups prune butter
3 x 20 cm length sprigs of myrtle or 6 fresh bay leaves
650 ml (+ extra) apple cider or apple juice
125 ml strong black coffee
¼ cup Chinese black vinegar or balsamic vinegar
16 pieces of dehydrated apple slices or 8 tbsp dried apple, roughly chopped

SERVES 8

PRUNE BUTTER

Combine all of the ingredients in a saucepan except for the brown sugar. Stir and bring to a gentle simmer and cook with the lid on for 20 minutes, stirring every few minutes. Remove the lid and continue to simmer and stir for 3 to 5 minutes until approximately 3 tbsp of liquid remains. Stir in the brown sugar and when dissolved, puree with a stick blender to a coarse consistency.

DEHYDRATED APPLE

Leaving the peel on and core in, cross-cut the apples into 5 mm slices and place on dehydrator racks. Following the manufacturers instructions, dry the sliced apple until a soft leather texture. Store in sealed containers.

PORK SHOULDER

Preheat oven to 220 °C. If the pork rind is still attached lay the pork shoulder flat with the skin side up on a clean work surface and score using a sharp knife or razor. Turn the pork over and season well. Thickly spread the prune butter over and into the muscle pockets. Reserving a little myrtle for garnish, lay the sprigs of myrtle or bay leaves on top and tightly roll.

RECIPE CONTINUES >

Tie with cotton kitchen string to secure. Place the pork on a metal cooling rack covered in aluminium foil with a few holes pressed through the foil to allow excess fat to drain. Pour the apple cider in to the bottom of the dish. Roast in the preheated oven for 25 minutes before reducing the temperature to 180 °C and cooking for 2 ½ hours. Check periodically to ensure there is still liquid in the bottom of the roasting tray. You may need to top it up with extra apple cider or water to keep a 1 cm depth of liquid. Remove from the oven, cover loosely with aluminium foil and rest for 30 minutes.

If the pork rind is not attached, lay the pork shoulder flat on a clean work surface and season both sides. Thickly spread the prune butter over and into the muscle pockets on the inside side of the shoulder. Reserving a little myrtle for garnish, lay the sprigs of myrtle or bay leaves on top and tightly roll. Tie with cotton kitchen string to secure. Gently and evenly brown the pork shoulder in a heavy-based deep roasting pan in nut-brown butter. Deglaze with the apple cider and transfer to the preheated oven to cook for 25 minutes. Remove from the oven, cover the pork with baking paper and then the whole roasting dish with a double layer of aluminium foil and return to a 180 °C oven for 3 hours. Remove the aluminium foil and leave to rest for 30 minutes.

For both recipe versions, transfer the rested pork to a plate and loosely cover with foil. Skim the fat from the surface of the cooking juices before bringing to a simmer. Add the coffee and simmer and stir until just starting to turn a syrup-like consistency. Stir through the black vinegar and taste, adjusting with a little extra apple cider if needing more sweetness to balance with the acid of the vinegar and lighten the sauce if too reduced and strong in flavour.

Carve the pork shoulder and serve with the sauce and crackling if included. Garnish with the dehydrated apple and reserved myrtle sprigs.

POTATOES

GLEN & DEAN RYAN

Spud growing in the Southern Forests has nearly a century of progression. From hand digging and carting with horse and dray, to the rail head at Bridgetown, to today's B-trains hauling 40% of Western Australia's total production to market, potatoes have long been a vital primary industry for our region.

Brothers Glen and Dean Ryan have been growing potatoes for the fresh market on their family farm east of Pemberton for over 30 years, with a current annual harvest of 3,500 tonne.

Along with changes to transport, the methods by which the Ryans have grown potatoes have developed and improved. 'We started remedial soil work 15 to 16 years ago with some success, and then 8 years ago, when we again noticed reductions in the quality, we made significant changes to build the soil ecology, providing balance and better soil structure. In the last 2 years we've seen a profound difference that has also helped greatly reduce the chemical fertilizer inputs,' Glen explains.

One constant aspect to the fresh potato industry (separate to the processing, seed and export sectors) is how it has been organised through a regulatory licensing system managed by the Potato Marketing Corporation of Western Australia. Each year, growers renew an initially purchased license to supply a determined amount at a specific time of the year. They can choose from many varieties within the three basic categories of red, blue and white-skinned potatoes.

'There is more flexibility than what some perceptions of this system have been, achieving supply that is very closely aligned with demand resulting in little wastage. Disease and issues that affect quality are also closely monitored, which is a great positive for our industry,' says Glen.

There is another myth that this system of potato-industry management limits choice, but Glen explains, 'Supermarkets have limited shelf space, which they divide up between red, blue and white potatoes, along with either brushed or washed. Some varieties are constant like the Royal Blues but others, which are not labelled by variety, are selected for similar traits but stocked on the shelves under those basic supermarket generic categories.'

With a mindset of innovation and progression, Glen and Dean have grown up to thirty-two varieties of potatoes in any one year and have found the Laura potato to be greatly successful for both its wonderful eating qualities and favourable response in the field. Red-skinned and oval-shaped with a yellow flesh and buttery rich flavour, the Laura potato was first recognised in 1998 in Germany and proved to be an all-rounder suitable for baking, roasting and mashing.

Asked, as a grower, what he would like consumers to think about when considering potatoes, Glen advises, 'Look beyond the cosmetic appearance, buy for quality, which also includes the dirt, and buy for taste! Experiment and get to know different varieties by asking the vegetable section manager or grocer for information and look for Southern Forests!'

KEFIR IS an ancient fermented milk drink that is laden with probiotics and has a mildly sour, yeasty taste. It is best prepared with kefir grains, which is a living culture of yeasts and bacteria. However, a powdered kefir starter is more easily obtainable; it can be purchased from health food stores or specialised gourmet food stores. If you don't have any facilities as described in this method to prepare coals to bake the potatoes, dry bake directly on the rack in a 200 °C preheated oven until soft enough to pierce with a paring knife.

COAL-BAKED POTATOES, KEFIR CREAM, PORCINI SALT & CORNICHONS

500 ml Bannister Downs Fresh Cream
1 sachet dried kefir powder
½ cup dried porcini mushrooms
2 tbsp salt flakes
12 sml waxy variety potatoes
e.g Laura, Royal Blue
12 cornichons
(pickled baby cucumbers)

SERVES 4 AS A SIDE DISH

Allow the cream to come to room temperature in a bowl before whisking in the dried kefir powder. Leave covered at room temperature for a minimum of 24 hours to gently ferment. Chill uncovered for a minimum of 4 hours. This will allow a thin crust to form on the surface of the kefir cream.

Grind the dried porcinis in an electric spice mill until a fine powder and then combine with the salt flakes.

Safely build a small fire in the base of a barbecue kettle or in a potbelly-style combustion heater until you have a small pile of hot coals. The coals must be hot but black in colour, not red hot. Make a well inside the pile of coals and put in the potatoes. Cover with the coals and leave to cook for 20 to 30 minutes. The cooking time will vary but keep checking every 10 minutes after 20 minutes has elapsed. Remove the potatoes and leave to cool slightly before dusting off the excess ash. Serve the potatoes halved with a large bowl of the kefir cream, small bowl of porcini salt and cornichons on the side.

THIS RECIPE is a quicker version of the traditional Barossa Streuselkuchen, which is a yeast cake base topped with fresh fruit and a sweet crunchy crumble. The mashed potato makes the cake moist and helps to bind the ingredients without the use of eggs. Use gin if schnapps or grappa is unavailable.

GERMAN POTATO & CURRANT CAKE WITH PEAR SCHNAPPS

Potato & Currant Cake

1 cup currants
½ cup pear schnapps or other fruit-based grappa
1 cup cooled mashed potato
1 ½ cups caster sugar
1 lemon, the zest finely grated
1 whole nutmeg, finely grated
4 cups self-raising flour
1 ½ cups buttermilk
icing sugar, to dust

Crumble

360 g plain flour
180 g caster sugar
1 tsp baking powder
1 tsp ground cinnamon
1 tsp vanilla extract
250 g unsalted butter, chilled & coarsely grated

SERVES 16

To make the crumble, combine the dry ingredients in a large bowl and then rub the grated butter and vanilla extract into the mixture until a coarse, crumbly texture. Place the crumble in the freezer until very cold. Store any leftover crumble in the freezer.

To make the cake, soak the currants in the schnapps overnight or heat in the microwave in a covered container until the currants have absorbed most of the schnapps. Preheat oven to 180 °C and line a lamington tray with baking paper.

Beat the mashed potato together with the caster sugar, lemon zest and grated nutmeg. Alternately and slowly add the self-raising flour and buttermilk to make a smooth cake batter. Fold in the currant mixture and spoon into the lamington tray, smoothing the surface evenly.

Thickly scatter a 1 cm layer of crumble over the surface of the batter before baking in the oven for 40 to 45 minutes until the crumble is golden and a skewer comes away clean when inserted into the middle of the cake. Leave to cool before dusting with icing sugar.

GREAT TO make with children and best made and eaten on the same day, these gluten-free flatbreads look and taste wonderful when also drizzled with extra virgin olive oil.

POTATO & BUCKWHEAT FLATBREAD

300 g mashed potato, cooled
100 g buckwheat flour
1 large free-range egg
salt flakes

SERVES 4

Preheat oven to 220 °C. Mix the mashed potato, buckwheat flour and egg with a pinch of salt until a soft dough. Divide into four portions and place on a lined baking tray. Flatten each with flour-dusted fingers into round disks, prick the breads with a fork and bake for 20 minutes until the edges are browned. Serve sprinkled with a little salt flakes.

PUMPKIN

JOHN KILRAIN

Pumpkins can commonly be seen on roadside stalls throughout the Southern Forests region. Many growers will plant pumpkins during the year in addition to their main product or crops. With supply and demand fluctuating from year to year and affecting the price, their sheds can either be full or empty at the end of the season. If full, the small investment to grow is a minimal loss. If empty, the small investment has netted a favourable gain.

John Kilrain is a part-time grower of pumpkins. He also farms corn and turf, which up until two years ago was his main source of income. A back injury has forced him away from heavier farming duties and more recently he has undertaken work as a real estate agent in Manjimup.

John's father, Michael, at 79 years old is still fit, strong and actively involved in the farming of their 160-acre property on the west side of Manjimup, 100 acres of which are under bluegum plantation. 'Once the region strengthens in terms of its ability to market its products, create demand and command better prices, there will be greater incentives for farming, not bluegum plantations as we've had to do in the past,' says John.

In their fourth consecutive pumpkin-growing year, John and Michael harvest their Waltham butternut and Sampson pumpkins from late February until mid-April, producing up to 100 tonne per year. Both varieties store well and can be sent to market at varying stages until mid October. 'We're busy for one month, but if other things are more urgent, we can leave what we need to do today until tomorrow without compromising quality,' John explains.

Many American cookbooks will specify canned pumpkin. As pumpkin is native to North America, the Native American tribes brought them as gifts to the European settlers who were reported to be initially unimpressed. When scurvy and exposure due to the harsh winters claimed many, they reassessed this versatile life-saving vegetable, creating the famous pumpkin pie 50 years after the first Thanksgiving.

Pumpkin's versatility for both sweet and savoury dishes makes it a wonderful all-rounder in the kitchen throughout the year. Choosing the Waltham butternut marginally over the Sampson, John enjoys it most in the classic winter staple pumpkin soup, and in the years when prices are high, there's even greater reason to enjoy its deliciously sweet taste.

BAKED DONUTS are, arguably, just as delicious as the traditional deep-fried ones and in this version they are made even healthier with the addition of wholemeal spelt flour and pumpkin puree.

SPELT & SPICED PUMPKIN DONUTS WITH CINNAMON SUGAR

Donuts

150 g plain flour
80 g wholemeal spelt flour
1 ½ tsp baking powder
½ tsp salt
1 tsp ground cinnamon
½ tsp ground nutmeg
⅓ cup grapeseed or vegetable oil
½ cup rapadura or soft brown sugar
1 free-range egg
1 ½ tsp vanilla extract
¾ cup pumpkin puree
½ cup milk

Coating

⅓ cup rapadura or
golden caster sugar
1 tsp ground cinnamon

MAKES 12

DONUTS

Preheat oven to 180 °C. Butter a 12 cup donut baking tray and set aside. Combine the flours, baking powder, salt and spices together. Beat the oil, rapadura sugar, egg, vanilla, pumpkin puree and milk in an electric mixer until combined. Slowly add the dry ingredients into the mixture and stir until just blended.

Using a pastry bag, pipe into each donut cup until half full with the batter. Bake for 10 to 15 minutes, until donuts spring back when gently pressed. Turn donuts onto a wire rack and allow to cool for a few minutes.

COATING

While the donuts are cooling, combine the rapadura sugar and ground cinnamon and then evenly dust the donuts until well covered. Serve while warm.

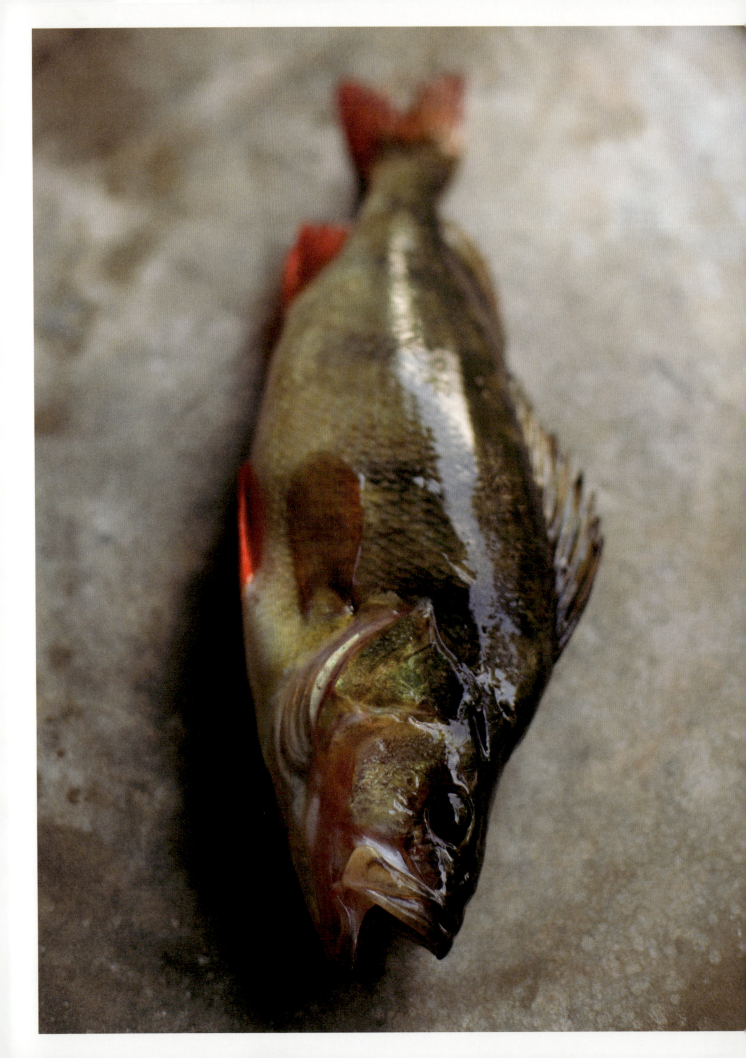

REDFIN PERCH

PAT STUBBERFIELD

In the era of sustainability, resourcefulness has been a key element to supporting the longevity of our natural environment. Biological foreigners to the natural cycles within our ecosystems have been introduced for various reasons throughout our state's history, often with unforeseen consequences. Redfin perch was released into natural waterways in Australia for sport and as a food source, but now, some 120 years later, is considered a noxious fish.

Seven redfin perch used as brood stock were delivered into the Ballarat Hatchery in Victoria from England in the late 1860s. The progeny from these fish were later released into Lake Powell near Albany, the Helena River in Guilford and Lake Monger in Perth in 1892, followed by the Capel, Preston and Blackwood rivers a few years later. Since then, they have spread into nearly all freshwater catchment dams and rivers in the south-west of Western Australia.

Redfin perch are prolific breeders and voracious predators with a very large mouth. They inhabit still or slow-flowing freshwater abundant with vegetation, crustaceans, worms, frogs, small fish and insect larvae. The waterways and dams in the Southern Forests are rich with this food and have been a perfect environment for the redfin perch to flourish.

Despite being aware of the benefits to native fish and marron of removing this predatory feral species, Pat Stubberfield's focus on fishing for redfin perch has been mainly for its eating qualities, seeing it as a potential product for the restaurant and retail trade.

A keen and competitive fisherman since he was a young boy growing up in Manjimup, Pat describes the taste of redfin perch as similar to Breaksea cod and having a very mild taste without the damp-fishiness often associated with freshwater fish. Pat enjoys it best simply crumbed and eaten hot, or cold for lunch the following day.

Many of the local landholders are keen to see the population of redfin perch in their dams reduced, so Pat's a welcome angler. Being able to access an abundant supply prompted Pat to consider turning this pest into a business opportunity, and over the past few years he has attempted to do so. Having encountered many obstacles to marketing the fish and with limited success, Pat has also continued operating a sports shop in Manjimup and now works fly-in fly-out in the construction industry while his wife, Anne, offers short-term accommodation in Manjimup at 'The Whitehouse'.

Pat still dreams of seeing redfin perch on menus and in fish shops. Success would provide further diversity to our plates and a reduction of the pressure that this attractive but lethal fish puts on native fish and crustacean species.

BAKING FRESHWATER fish in a salt crust insulates the flesh and keeps it moist while seasoning it at the same time, without becoming too salty. Skordalia is a puree of Greek origin that is heavily flavoured with garlic, and vinegar or lemon juice and thickened with ground nuts, potato and/or bread. A delicious accompaniment to baked or grilled fish.

ROSEMARY SALT–BAKED REDFIN PERCH WITH ALMOND SKORDALIA

Rosemary Salt–Baked Redfin Perch

1 x 600 g whole redfin perch, gutted & scaled
3 free-range egg whites
6 cups coarse rock salt
⅓ cup rosemary, finely chopped
4 sprigs rosemary, stripped
1 lemon, sliced
8 fresh bay leaves
extra virgin olive oil
1 lemon, cut into wedges

Almond Skordalia

1 free-range egg yolk
¼ cup lemon juice
3 cloves garlic, finely chopped
⅓ cup almond meal
¾ cup fresh sourdough breadcrumbs
½ cup extra virgin olive oil
2 tbsp (+ extra) water
sea salt flakes & freshly cracked black pepper

SERVES 2

ROSEMARY SALT–BAKED REDFIN PERCH

Preheat oven to 220 °C. Combine the salt, egg whites, chopped and stripped rosemary until the texture of damp sand. Place a 2 cm thick layer on the bottom of a baking tray, slightly larger than the dimensions of the redfin perch. Stuff the cavity with the sliced lemon and two of the bay leaves. Wrap the remaining bay leaves around the outside of the fish and lay on the salt. Pile the remaining salt mixture over the top of the fish, patting it down to ensure the fish is evenly covered. Bake for 20 to 25 minutes. Using a meat thermometer, pierce into the thickest part of the fish. When 60 °C the fish is cooked. Remove the top layer of salt, drizzle with extra virgin olive oil, and serve with lemon wedges and a bowl of Almond Skordalia.

ALMOND SKORDALIA

Blend the egg yolk, lemon juice and garlic in a food processor for 10 to 15 seconds. Add the almond meal and breadcrumbs and then, with the motor running, slowly pour in the olive oil and enough water to make a thick mayonnaise-like consistency. Season to taste.

SAFFRON

TERRY MACFARLANE

The Southern Forests region is now well known for the prized black truffle; however, there is another small, rare and highly valuable gourmet food product grown here. It's saffron.

Being a qualified agronomist doesn't necessarily preclude being a successful farmer; however, holding a PhD in botany when considering saffron production has certainly been of great advantage for Terry Macfarlane.

Terry spent his childhood in Pemberton, leaving to study botany in Perth. After returning to the region, Terry obtained a handful of Crocus sativus quorms from the only Australian commercial saffron grower, in Tasmania, planting them as a trial at the back of his west Manjimup property in 1996.

With a karri loam soil, secure water availability, and a temperate climate similar to that of the Mediterranean and parts of the Middle East where saffron has been grown for centuries, the planting went well. Terry has successfully extended his initial planting through patient bulb division and replanting.

Saffron production is incredibly labour intensive and therefore it is the most expensive spice in the world. No parts of the planting, growing, harvesting, processing and packing methods have been mechanised. To produce 1 kg of saffron, the stigmas (also called filaments) of nearly a quarter of a million flowers need to be hand picked.

Terry's saffron flowers for approximately two weeks towards the end of April, during which he and his family pick the flowers in the early morning, and separate the stigmas with their fingertips, after which they are dried, intensifying the colour, flavour and providing shelf life. They are then packaged in ½ gram sachets and, so far, have mostly been sold to the local Filipino community in Manjimup and Sri Lankan community in Perth.

Saffron has a long and rich heritage as a food plant, preceded by its use as a medicinal remedy and dye during prehistoric times. It has a distinctive woody aroma of dried hay and honey with a slightly bitter taste and has commonly been used in French bouillabaisse, Spanish paella, Milanese risotto, Indian rice dishes, celebratory bread in Sweden, and traditional cakes and breads in England.

While Terry and his family will continue the painstaking effort needed to produce this unique and historic spice, they also need a second income stream. Terry's day job as a senior research scientist with the Department of Parks and Wildlife in Manjimup allows him to continue to live and work in this abundant and diverse food region in Western Australia.

THIS IS a traditional recipe that's often called a cake but is more like a sweet bread due to yeast being the raising agent. Despite saffron being grown in other parts of England, the Cornish apparently traded tin with foreign merchants, who were possibly Phoenicians, for it as early as 400 BC. When you taste the result you'll no doubt agree it was pretty good trade!

CORNISH SAFFRON BREAD

Cornish Saffron Bread

300 ml milk
1 tsp saffron threads
15 g fresh yeast or 2 tsp dried yeast
60 g caster sugar
500 g plain strong flour
1 tsp salt
¼ tsp freshly grated nutmeg
1 tsp ground cinnamon
1 tsp mixed spice
125 g unsalted butter, softened
100 g currants

For the Glaze

2 tbsp milk
2 tbsp caster sugar

To Serve

Bannister Downs double cream

MAKES 2 SML LOAVES

Warm a quarter cup of the milk and stir through the saffron threads. Leave for a minimum of 1 hour. Warm another quarter cup of the milk and stir through the yeast with half a teaspoon of the sugar. Leave for 10 to 15 minutes until frothy.

Place the flour, remaining sugar, salt and spices into a mixing bowl and then rub the butter in with your fingertips until well combined. Warm the remaining milk. Make a well in the flour mixture and then stir in the yeast mixture, the saffron mixture and warm milk until a rough lumpy dough forms. Scatter over the currants before tipping out on to a lightly floured surface. Knead until silky and smooth, about 10 minutes.

Place the dough in a lightly oiled bowl, cover with a plastic film and leave in a warm place to rise for a couple of hours.

Grease and line two 23.5 x 7.5 cm bar cake pans with baking paper. Turn out the dough onto a lightly floured surface, divide into two portions and gently shape before placing in the tins. Cover and leave in a warm place for about an hour.

Bake in a preheated 190 °C oven for 25 to 30 minutes. Warm the milk and sugar for the glaze, stirring to make sure the sugar dissolves. As soon as you take the tea bread out of the oven, brush with the glaze. Leave to stand in the tin for 15 minutes, then turn out and leave to cool completely before serving with Bannister Downs double cream.

SAUSAGES

THE SOUTHERNERS FOOTBALL CLUB

Each year from the end of May through to July – when the weather is cool but not yet soaking wet, and the flies are long gone – local farming families across the region undertake the tradition of killing a pig to make all manner of preserved meats, including sausages to dry or eat fresh, as their pioneering ancestors did before them.

In Pemberton, the local Italian families also started this tradition many years ago as a fundraising exercise for the Sacred Heart Catholic Church and St Joseph's Catholic Primary School. Later, this fundraising method was adopted for their other extended community family, The Southerners Football Club.

Justin Omodei, the president of the club, explains, 'It started some 30 years ago with the Bendotti Barbecue. After a church service, which was held on Palm Sunday in a shed belonging to the Bendotti family, links of fresh sausages were auctioned off. They were sought after by the local townsfolk who couldn't do it themselves. All the Dings were involved: the Agostinis, the Bendottis, the Decampos, the Della Francas, the Della Golas, the Della Vadovas, Moltonis and us Omodeis together with the Parolins, O'Connells and Scotmans.'

The sausage making is now always led by the senior statesman of the club. 'Joe Bendotti was awarded best and fairest in 1980 and is now in charge of the day. The pig is donated and all the labour offered with great community spirit.'

Now undertaken two or three times a year by the club, on farms for personal use and in the club's commercial kitchen for auction, the professionally organised process taking several days always starts with the detailed clean down of heavy-duty commercial equipment.

After being dispatched, the pig is left to hang in the coolroom for two days. Eighty-something year old Southerners' runner and retired butcher Hedley Green divides the pork into primary cuts and then, with others assisting, prepares the meat into smaller chunks. It is then seasoned with a special ratio of salt, pepper, garlic, spices and red wine before being minced and then cased into sausages using natural skins.

The remaining bones are roasted and simmered with local potatoes, eaten with fresh bread and enjoyed with homemade wine or beer for lunch. 'Nothing is wasted and all generations are involved,' Justin explains, 'the club is a big extended family. We love the football side of things, but it's really the people that are the most important.'

Community traditions such as this are the highlights, through an active year, of a historical network of interlinked families that are the backbone of all of the towns in the Southern Forests region. This is the legacy of pioneering days, when survival critically depended on always caring for and supporting others during difficult times, the spirit of which remains the foundation upon which the region continues to build.

THIS IS Joe Bendotti's master sausage recipe, which he prepares at least six times, for separate groups, throughout the sausage-making season. Naturally, there's a certain flick of the wrist when it comes to tying the sausage links, so you may need a demonstration from your butcher to get you started!

JOE BENDOTTI'S FRESH ITALIAN SAUSAGES

4 bulbs garlic, the cloves
peeled & crushed

1 ½ king brown beer bottles
(approx. 1.125 litres) red wine

10 tbsp cracked pepper

2 tbsp ground cinnamon

2 dessertspoons ground cloves

2 tsp chilli powder

2 tsp ground nutmeg

900 g salt

45 kg large-diced pork

natural sausage skins,
soaked in cold water

MAKES MANY KILOS

Mix the crushed garlic and red wine together in a bowl. Evenly sprinkle all the spices and salt over the pork, which has been laid out over a large, deep stainless steel tray. Gently massage through to evenly distribute.

Strain the red wine through a tea towel while evenly pouring over the spiced meat. Take a quarter of the crushed garlic remaining in the tea towel and gently mix into the meat with the wine before putting through a coarse mincer.

Group the mince in small amounts, which will make putting it through the sausage filler easier. Use natural sausage skins and cotton string to form sausages to desired length.

BUCKWHEAT POLENTA is a very traditional dish from the Valtellina region in the north of Italy that many of the descendants of the original migrant families still prepare on sausage making day. They pour it directly onto a serving board in the middle of the table for the crowd of hungry helpers to enjoy.

ITALIAN SAUSAGES WITH BUCKWHEAT POLENTA, CRISPY SAGE LEAVES AND BURNT BUTTER

125 g coarse polenta
60 g buckwheat flour
1 ½ tsp salt
1 litre full cream milk
250 g unsalted butter
50 g Italian Parmesan, finely grated
6 coarse Italian-style fresh sausages
1 cup fresh sage leaves

SERVES 4

Combine polenta, buckwheat flour and salt. Bring the milk to simmer in a large saucepan. Remove from the heat. Slowly pour in the polenta mix while whisking. When smooth, place a simmer mat on the burner and return to a low heat. Cook for 20 minutes while stirring regularly to prevent sticking and burning. Stir in 25 g of the unsalted butter and Parmesan and keep covered and warm on the side.

Place the fresh coarse Italian-style sausages in a saucepan and cover with cold water. Very gently bring to a simmer and allow to slowly cook for 8 to 10 minutes. Turn the heat off and leave the sausages another 5 minutes before draining.

Place the 200 g unsalted butter in a frypan and cook until a nutty brown colour, swirling the butter in the pan as it starts to brown. Add the sage leaves and fry for 2 to 3 minutes until crisp.

If needed, stir a little hot water into the buckwheat polenta to loosen before pouring it onto a platter. Thickly slice the sausages and arrange on top before pouring over the burnt butter and serving with the crispy sage leaves.

TROUT

PAUL THOMSETT

Given the ready supply of timber, most pioneering families in the Southern Forests region constructed their homes from hand-felled, sawn and split logs. General decay with time, white ant attack, fire or demolition has left little evidence of these early dwellings; however, a few homes that were built from bricks made of local clay still remain. Clover Cottage was built for Peter and Ellen Wheatley in 1875 near the Warren River, approximately 30 km south of Manjimup.

Current owners Paul and Petrina Thomsett moved into Clover Cottage homestead in 1983. After extensive renovations and the construction of several holiday chalets, and dams for recreational fishing, the property is now a tourism business operating as Clover Cottage Country Retreat.

Paul's electronic engineering background and natural building skills enabled him to develop a small trout-breeding facility for the purposes of stocking their dams. These dams now attract many keen fly-fishing enthusiasts and supply local farmers with trout fry for their personal dams.

Trout is not a native Australian fish. A handful of rainbow trout were first released into the Eastbrook Stream in 1931 by schoolteacher C.A Glew as a school project. Having found some surviving trout a few years later, the Trout Acclimatization Society was formed. Breeding ponds were built in Pemberton, and ongoing yearly release into waterways continued for recreational fishing and to encourage further tourism in the area.

The ponds and program were handed over to the Department of Fisheries in 1976, who continued with research, and breeding and releasing programs. The Pemberton Trout Hatchery was then built, extending on from the original breeding ponds, and was again refurbished in 1998. Through selective breeding over the years, trout at the now Pemberton Freshwater Research Centre have adapted to slightly warmer temperatures than their natural 5 to 20 °C requirement, making them unique to the Southern Forests region.

Each year, both rainbow and brown trout species are released into south-west public dams and the Collie, Blackwood, Donnelly and Warren rivers for more than 8,000 recreational fly fishing and angling enthusiasts. If they're not caught and they don't suffer lower oxygen levels due to heat and water stagnation, trout can reach 2 kg in two years.

The endearing Irish heritage and pioneering spirit of the original owners of Clover Cottage, Peter and Ellen Wheatley, can be easily felt when visiting and staying at the beautifully preserved example of local history that is Clover Cottage Country Retreat. Along with marroning, trout fishing was probably one of the first food tourism experiences in the Southern Forests and is arguably still a culinary asset to our naturally abundant and diverse region.

COULIBIAC IS of Russian origin, traditionally made with fresh salmon. Usually it includes boiled eggs; however, this trout version is no less good for their absence. Although there are a few components to prepare for this celebratory dish, your time and efforts will be greatly rewarded.

TROUT COULIBIAC WITH SOUR CREAM

Wild Rice, Leek & Mushroom Mixture

½ cup wild rice
230 g leek, roughly chopped
300 g field mushrooms, halved & thinly sliced
50 g unsalted butter
sea salt & freshly cracked black pepper
2 tbsp fresh dill, finely chopped

Buckwheat Crêpes

70 g buckwheat flour
100 g plain flour
¼ tsp salt
450 ml full cream milk
3 free-range eggs
butter, for frying

Trout Coulibiac

1 sheet Carême puff pastry
sea salt & freshly cracked black pepper
2 lrg trout fillets, pin bones removed
1 free-range egg
2 tbsp milk
sour cream, to serve
dill sprigs, for garnish

SERVES 6 – 8

WILD RICE, LEEK & MUSHROOM MIXTURE

Soak the rice overnight or for a minimum of 4 hours. Drain and cook in boiling salted water for 30 minutes until tender. Drain. Gently fry the leeks and mushrooms in the butter with seasoning until all the juices have evaporated. Fold through the cooked rice and cool before stirring through the fresh dill. Refrigerate.

BUCKWHEAT CRÊPES

To make the buckwheat crêpes, place the dry ingredients into a bowl and make a well. Beat the milk and eggs together, pour into the well and gradually whisk into the dry ingredients to make a batter the consistency of rich pouring cream. Using a non-stick or crêpe pan, drop a small piece of butter into the hot pan and wipe with a paper towel. Pour ¼ cup batter into the pan and swirl to cover evenly. After a minute, place a wide thin spatula or palette knife under the crêpe and carefully flip over. Cook the other side for 30 seconds and then slide onto a plate. Place a piece of baking paper roughly the same size as the crêpe on top and repeat using all the batter.

TROUT COULIBIAC

Roll the pastry out until half the given thickness. Cut the pastry in half and measure to ensure the length and width of each piece is approximately 2 to 3 cm larger than the trout fillet. Line a large baking tray with baking paper. RECIPE CONTINUES >

Place one piece of the pastry on the tray and then lay some of the crêpes on the pastry, overlapping to completely cover the pastry. Spoon half the wild rice mixture down the middle of the crêpe layer, to the approximate width of the trout fillet and within 3 cm of the length. Season the trout fillet before laying it on the wild rice mixture, placing the thicker end of the second trout fillet on top of the thinner end of the first trout fillet. Cover with the remaining wild rice mixture before overlapping the crêpes to cover. Use any leftover crêpes to fill any missing gaps.

Beat the egg and milk together to make an egg wash. Brush around the edges of the bottom piece of pastry and then lay the other piece of pastry on top of the crêpe-covered trout. Crimp the edges together with your fingertips or press with the tines of a fork. Egg wash the top and gently crosshatch a pattern onto the surface with the tip of a paring knife. Refrigerate while preheating your oven to 220 °C.

Bake for 20 minutes. Reduce the temperature to 180 °C and bake a further 10 to 15 minutes until a golden colour.

Leave for 5 minutes before slicing and garnishing with fresh dill sprigs and serving with sour cream.

IT MAY seem a little odd to have small shortbread biscuits in a salad, but they add a lovely soft buttery crunch that complements the pepperiness of the watercress and smoky soft texture of the hot smoked trout. You can also serve these biscuits with drinks as a lovely starter.

WATERCRESS LEAVES & EMULSION, FLAKED HOT SMOKED TROUT, YOGHURT & MUSTARD SEED BISCUITS

Mustard Seed Biscuits

225 g plain flour
150 g unsalted butter
100 g sharp vintage cheddar
½ tsp black mustard seeds
1 free-range egg yolk

Hot Smoked Trout

3.8 litres water
340 g salt
⅔ cup white sugar
1 bay leaf
1 tbsp black peppercorns
1 lrg fresh trout
hickory, mesquite or other fragrant wood chips or sawdust for smoking
vegetable oil

SERVES 4

MUSTARD SEED BISCUITS

Combine the ingredients in a food processor and pulse until the mixture just starts to adhere together. Divide the biscuit dough into two and, using aluminum foil, roll into 3 ½ cm diameter cylinders. Preheat oven to 180 °C and line baking trays with baking paper. Chill for 20 minutes before slicing into 1 cm thick slices. Lay on baking trays and bake for 20 to 25 minutes until golden. Cool on a wire cooling rack.

HOT SMOKED TROUT

Place the salt, sugar, peppercorns and bay leaf in a small saucepan and pour over enough of the water to cover. Bring to a simmer, stirring to dissolve salt and sugar before combining with the remaining water in a deep tray long enough for the trout. Submerge the trout, using a smaller tray or plates to keep the trout under the level of the water. Place in the fridge overnight. Next day, remove the trout and wrap in a tea towel to dry. Leave the trout for up to an hour to air and completely dry while preparing the hot smoker. Following the manufacturer's instructions, preheat the charcoal and boil water for the waterbath. Put the wood chips on top of the coals and then place the waterbath on top. Lightly oil the trout before laying it on the racks above the now smoking and steaming base. Cover with lid and smoke for 30 to 40 minutes. RECIPE CONTINUES >

Emulsion

100 g watercress, washed
& roughly chopped

100 ml grapeseed oil

2 tsp Dijon mustard

½ tsp sugar

sea salt flakes & freshly
cracked black pepper

2 – 3 tbsp water

To Serve

2 lrg handfuls fresh
watercress, washed

½ cup natural yoghurt

3 – 4 mustard seeds biscuits
per person

¼ lrg hot smoked trout, off the bone
& flaked into chunks

black mustard seeds, to garnish

4 lemon wedges, to serve

SERVES 4

The temperature should be around 70 °C. Check the inside of the trout for a light pink/rose colour and the skin should be golden and burnished. Using your fingers, gently slip the trout flesh off the bone, taking care to remove the pin bones.

EMULSION

Using a stick or strong bench top blender, puree all the ingredients until smooth, adding more water if needed to make a sauce the consistency of runny cream.

TO SERVE

Gently break the watercress into bite-sized lengths and divide onto four plates. Place spoonfuls of the emulsion in between the leaves, before topping with the smoked trout and mustard biscuits. Spoon a little yoghurt in small amounts on top of the salad and scatter over a few mustard seeds to garnish. Serve each with a lemon wedge.

TRUFFLES

DAVID POTTINGER

In a similar way that the black truffle saved the vignerons in Périgord France due to the outbreak of phylloxera in the late 1870s, growing truffles has provided a successful step forward for David Pottinger and his family following the decline in demand for grapes in Australia.

Born in Kirkwall, Orkney in the north of Scotland, David spent his first years on Strongsay Island before migrating to Wyalkatchem via Cowaramup in 1968, where his parents David, and Alma, farmed wheat and sheep for 13 years. The family then relocated to Pemberton in 1981, recognising the opportunities for agricultural diversification due to the Mediterranean climate and productive soils.

After entering into tertiary education to study geology, David returned to the farm in preference over a city school desk. At 21 he started a four-year saw-docking apprenticeship at the Pemberton timber mill that was followed by a five-year period in a mill in Northcliffe.

In 1987, David and his father planted vineyards, supplying grapes to Houghtons throughout the 1990s. Over a chat at Rotary with plant nurseryman Al Blakers, who was developing the beginnings of the truffle industry in Manjimup with mycology scientist Nick Malajczuk, David and his father decided to plant 1,000 inoculated hazelnut and oak trees on two steeply sloped hectares over a two-year period from 1999.

'For a few years we used to joke that it was just a beautiful paddock of hazelnuts and oaks,' David recalls. Their first year's truffle harvest of 4 kg in 2004 has now increased to 1.1 tonne in 2013 – the highest amount from a cultivated site in recorded history anywhere in the world. David and his father now agree that the beautiful paddock has proven itself more than a pretty view.

'As soon as a truffle breaks the surface, we cover them with sand to prevent sunburn and allow time for ripening. The truffle dog handler then marks the spot and we follow to carefully hand harvest with a trowel. After weighing, they're washed, graded and trimmed before being transported to one of several distributors,' David explains.

Despite the domestic market growing in the last 5 to 6 years, of the total 5 tonne of national truffle production in 2013, only 500 kg remained in the Australian market and the remainder was exported.

David's not absolutely certain why their site has provided such spectacular results in quantity and quality. He plans to further upgrade their processing with a truffle washing machine and continue to enjoy a farming life, with further diversifying plans for their beautiful Pemberton property.

WHEN SERVED as a side dish, this explosion of textural deep earthy flavours would best accompany a simple pork neck or veal shoulder braise. If served as a small starter, an Amontillado or Oloroso sherry would be a fine accompaniment.

ROASTED JERUSALEM ARTICHOKES, HAZELNUTS, TRUFFLE, LABNA & SAGE

500 g Greek yoghurt
1 tsp sea salt flakes
850 g Jerusalem artichokes, scrubbed
⅓ cup fresh sage leaves
1 cup roasted hazelnuts,
roughly chopped
extra virgin olive oil
salt flakes
1 tbsp verjuice
labna, scoop of
1 sml fresh black truffle
freshly cracked black pepper

SERVES 4 AS A SIDE DISH

Make the labna by stirring the salt through the yoghurt and draining in a muslin-lined strainer overnight in the refrigerator.

Preheat oven to 220 °C. Cut the larger Jerusalem artichokes in halves to ensure all are roughly the same size and will cook evenly. Scatter on a baking tray together with the sage leaves and hazelnuts. Drizzle over a little extra virgin olive oil and season with salt flakes. Roast in the oven for 30 minutes until the Jerusalem artichokes are golden and tender and the sage crispy. Evenly pour over the verjuice and shake the tray to loosely amalgamate. Serve on a platter with a scoop of labna in the middle, freshly cracked black pepper and generous shavings of fresh black truffle.

CROQUETTES ARE a perennial favourite and make a wonderful canapé during winter. The truffle mayonnaise and truffle salt deliver an extra punch of flavour and contribute to the holy trinity of salt, fat and crunch in this dish we all seem hard-wired to love.

MUSHROOM AND TRUFFLE CROQUETTES WITH TRUFFLE MAYONNAISE

Truffle Mayonnaise

200 ml grapeseed or vegetable oil

200 ml extra virgin olive oil

2 free-range egg yolks

1 free-range egg

1 tbsp white wine vinegar

2 tbsp lemon juice

1 tsp salt

½ cup boiling water

3 tbsp truffle oil

20 g fresh truffle, shaved

Mushroom & Truffle Croquettes

1 x 50 g pack dried mixed forest mushrooms

200 g Swiss brown mushrooms

50 g butter

45 g plain flour

250 ml full cream milk

100 g cheddar cheese, grated

½ tsp ground nutmeg

sea salt flakes and freshly ground black pepper

20 g fresh truffle, thinly sliced

2 free-range eggs, beaten

100 g Panko breadcrumbs

plain flour, to dust

sunflower oil for frying

truffle salt, to serve

MAKES 15

TRUFFLE MAYONNAISE

Combine the grapeseed and olive oils. Process the egg yolks, whole egg, vinegar and lemon juice and salt in a food processor until frothy. With the motor running, drizzle in the combined oils to make a thick mayonnaise. Add the boiling water and process again to make the mayonnaise light and fluffy. Process again with the truffle oil until combined. Season to taste and transfer to a bowl. Fold through the fresh truffle.

MUSHROOM & TRUFFLE CROQUETTES

Rehydrate the dried mushroom mixture in 1 ½ cups water for a minimum of 2 hours. Drain and reserve the soaking liquid. Dice the rehydrated mushrooms and Swiss brown mushrooms into small pieces. The combined weight should be approximately 500 g.

Heat a heavy-based medium saucepan over a medium high heat and add the butter. Once foaming add the mushrooms, season well and cook for at least 2 minutes. Strain the reserved wild-mushroom soaking liquid through a fine strainer into the saucepan. Cook until the mushrooms are wilted and tender and most of the liquid evaporated.

Add the flour and stir over the heat until the mixture is crumbly and dry. Add the milk, bit by bit, stirring as you add until you have a smooth paste. Add the grated cheese and ground nutmeg. Cook the mixture for a further 5 minutes. RECIPE CONTINUES >

Season to taste and then fold through the fresh truffle. Spread the mix into a shallow tray, place a piece of baking paper directly onto the surface of the mixture and refrigerate until firm and cold.

For the crumbing, place the beaten egg into a bowl and mix with 1 tbsp of water. Fill a separate bowl with flour and add the Panko crumbs into another bowl.

Using two spoons of the same size, quenelle the mushroom mix into cylinders. Dip the cylinders in the bowl of flour, shake off any excess then dip in the beaten egg, and finally the breadcrumbs, making sure that all the sides are completely covered. Repeat with the remaining mushroom mix. These can be left covered in the fridge until you are ready to fry them.

Fill a deep pan one-third full with sunflower oil. Once it has reached 180 °C fry the croquettes in batches until golden on all sides. Transfer to a plate lined with kitchen roll to drain.

Serve the croquettes immediately on a bed of truffle mayonnaise, sprinkled with truffle salt.

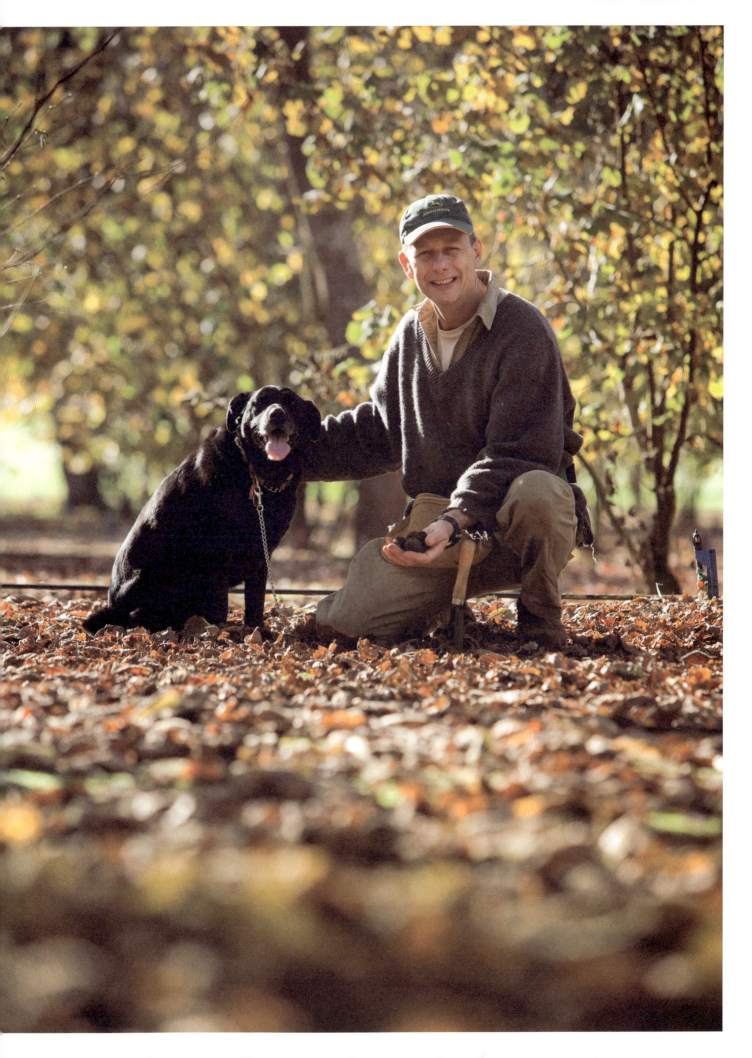

WILD MUSHROOMS

Experts have long agreed that Western Australia's south-west, with the Southern Forests region at its southerly heart, is one of the most botanically diverse locations in the world. Home to over 1,500 plant species (of which most are endemic), the towering karri, marri, tingle and jarrah forests also host a complex and mostly undiscovered world of fungi, above and below ground.

Fungi play a critical role in a healthy well-functioning ecosystem. According to the very informative field guide *Fungi of the South-West Forests* written by mycologist Dr Richard Robinson and published by the West Australian Department of Parks and Wildlife, there are at least ten times as many fungi as plants in Australia, with only 5% formally described and named, let alone classified as edible or poisonous.

Foraging has certainly become a popular foodie trend, the ultimate for many being the gathering of wild mushrooms. Every year, however, there are fatalities in Australia due to the death cap mushroom Amanita Phalloides as it is easily confused with a field mushroom.

In every field guide and from every expert, the warnings are loud and clear: never eat any wild mushroom before getting a positive sighted identification from an expert.

The gathering of any wild food also requires a permit. The effect of removing any fungi or plant material on other plants or animals needs to be considered and taken into account. Check the Department of Parks and Wildlife website for further details.

The following are possible examples of known edible species; however, to avoid uncertainty and potential misidentification, the photographs should not be used for identification purposes.

top. BEEFSTEAK FUNGUS FISTULINA HEPATICA

It's easy to see how this fungus gets its name; however, the slightly sour acidic taste is nothing like you'd imagine. In Europe this fungus grows on oak trees, but here in Western Australia it prefers jarrah. Cut surfaces take on a liver-red colour adding to the perceptions of its name.

bottom. HEDGEHOGS, HYDNUM REPANDUM

Hedgehogs or Wood Hedgehogs are characterised by their spines that appear on the underside of the caps instead of gills. They are a sought after edible fungi in Northern America and Europe; however, the Australian species is reported to be of inferior taste and texture.

top left. AUSTRALIAN HONEY FUNGUS, ARMILLARIA LUTEOBUBALINA

One of the local older Italian ladies in Pemberton identified this fungus as a local mushroom to the area she migrated from. It is parasitic and most commonly found in large clusters on the stems and at the base of dead trees or stumps.

top right. PINK CHANTARELLE, CANTHARELLUS AFF. CINNABARINUS VAR. AUSTRALIENSIS

Presently considered an Australian variety of the red chanterelle, they're found in groups poking their striking pink frilly heads through the brown leaf litter. They're reported to have a faint apricot smell and very bland taste.

bottom left. SLIPPERY JACKS, SUILLUS LUTEUS

This is an introduced fungus that's part of the bolete family, which is indigenous to coniferous forests in Europe and locally found in pine plantations. The cap is slimy and easily damaged and best wiped to prevent the possibility of indigestion.

bottom right. BLACK MOREL, MORCHELLA ELATA

There are several species of morels in Australia, but the black morel is the probably the only species found in the south-west. Distinctively characterised by their long vertical honeycomb-like ridges, they can be found in large numbers after bushfires. They require cooking to avoid digestive upsets, but unfortunately they're not as strongly flavoured as their highly sought-after European relative Morchella esculenta.

THIS WONDERFUL winter salad uses dried wild mushrooms, which are more easily obtainable than fresh but still deliver that wonderful forest-floor smell and taste. Kasza is pre-roasted and pre-steamed buckwheat kernels that can be found in gourmet grocery stores or health food shops. Quark is a fresh curd cheese with a pleasant sour tang; thick Greek yoghurt or labna can be used as a substitute.

TOASTED GRAINS & WILD MUSHROOM SALAD WITH QUARK

1 x 30 g pack dried
chanterelle mushrooms

1 x 30 g pack dried
wild forest mushrooms

½ litre water

½ cup kasza
(roasted buckwheat kernels)

½ cup red quinoa

½ cup freekah (roasted green wheat)

½ cup Puy lentils

1 leek, the white section thickly sliced

1 x field mushroom, thinly sliced

3 tbsp olive oil

½ litre mushroom or vegetable stock

1 lemon, the juice of

½ cup toasted almonds,
roughly chopped

¼ cup pepitas

¼ cup sunflower seeds

1 tbsp sesame seeds

1 lrg handful mixed salad greens &
herbs – sorrel, lovage, curly endive,
land or watercress, Italian parsley

salt flakes & freshly
cracked black pepper

quark, thick Greek yoghurt or labna,
to serve

1 tbsp truffle oil

SERVES 8

Combine and soak the dried chanterelle and wild forest mushrooms in the water overnight or for 2 to 3 hours. Cover the kasza with cold water and soak overnight or for 2 to 3 hours.

Lightly toast the quinoa in a dry frying pan before boiling in salted water for 10 minutes until tender. Drain, run under cold water to cool and drain well before transferring to a large bowl. Simmer the freekah and Puy lentils together in salted water for 20 to 30 minutes until tender, before running under cold water, straining and transferring to the bowl with the quinoa. Drain the soaked kasza and add to the other grains and lentils in the bowl.

Drain the soaked mixed dried mushrooms through a colander, reserving the soaking liquid. Strain this liquid through a fine sieve to remove any grit. Gently sauté the leek and field mushroom in the olive oil until softened. Toss through the soaked dried mushrooms before pouring over the mushroom liquid and mushroom stock. Simmer and reduce until the liquid volume only just covers the mushrooms and leeks. Leave to cool before stirring through the lemon juice.

Add the mushroom mixture to the grain mixture together with the almonds, pepitas, sunflower seeds and sesame seeds and then toss through the mixed salad greens and herbs. Season to taste, adding more lemon juice if required. Serve with a spoonful of quark per person and drizzle with a little truffle oil.

ABOUT THE AUTHOR

SOPHIE ZALOKAR was born and raised in the Barossa Valley in South Australia and trained as a chef under Australian food icon Maggie Beer at her and her husband Colin Beer's famed restaurant, The Pheasant Farm. She went on to travel and cook around the world, settling in Fremantle, Western Australia in 1990.

Her first book, PicNic – Outdoor Feasts in the Australian Landscape was short-listed for the Jacob's Creek World Food Media Awards and Vittoria Australian Food Media Awards in 2003. She has developed recipes for Homes and Living magazine and provided a weekly recipe in The West Australian newspaper for the past 11 years.

At the beginning of 2005, Sophie and her family moved from Fremantle to a 18 ½ acre smallholding with holiday cottages in Pemberton, within the Southern Forests region of Western Australia.

With the assistance of a federal tourism grant, Sophie and her husband Chris opened Foragers Field Kitchen & Cooking School in April 2011, offering residential cooking school and dinner events throughout the year, promoting the culinary heritage and produce grown in the Southern Forests.

Sophie's work as a chef, food writer, teacher and produce judge is underpinned by her commitment to nurturing real food created with a deep respect for the land, primary producers, and local food heritage and culinary traditions.

THANK YOU

For choosing to take an interest in one of Western Australia's best kept secrets. In the age of searching for authenticity, the Southern Forests is truly the antidote to concrete jungles and the disconnection from the natural world that comes from living in them.

Thank you to the Southern Forests Food Council who, in their infancy at the time, chose to support this project, for which I am grateful. Thank you for this rare opportunity to represent a little of the diversity and agricultural riches of our beautiful region that I've discovered over the past 10 years.

Particular thanks to Nic Giblett for your support. The legacy of your stewardship will no doubt be as pioneering and as significant as your forebears.

Naturally, having the chance to cook and write for a project like this could never have happened without the producers being there to start with. Their warm hospitality, generosity and kind support was and continues to be just wonderful, the debt for which weighed heavily on my conscience as the pans hit the heat and words hit the screen. I wish to sincerely thank them all.

Thank you also to my fungi-friend Peter, who randomly turns up throughout the season from the depths of the forest with something curiously interesting to muse over. Four out of six of the fungi in this book were from his knowledgeable sleuthing work.

Thank you to Joel Veech, whom I've actually never met, but who delivered fresh abalone directly into my cool room, scrubbed and ready to go, after a very quick chat on the phone via our mutual friend-of-the-sea, Judy Dittmer.

To John Della Franca for letting me rummage through your fabulous 'yard heaps' for the food photography backgrounds and for cutting that enormous marri slab. Thank goodness work safety officers weren't around and you lived another day to cut wood and grow buckwheat.

To Marianne Peyer, Alyssa Cowgill and Aki Kurosawa who helped with the food shoots. Your wonderful work in the kitchen has been memorable and such a support. Thank you!

Sincerest thanks to Craig Kinder of f22 Photography. Your professionalism, talent, disarming nature and willingness to go the extra mile to achieve a collaborative vision has made this book a beautiful gift that all Southern Forests locals can be proud to share with the world. Thank you for realising the great bounty and extraordinary beauty of this region through your stunning images.

Grateful thanks to the small and dedicated team at UWA Publishing. Thank you to Kate Pickard. Our shared love of seeing the natural beauty in places, people and food could not have appeared on these pages without your support on this project. Thank you also to Anna Maley-Fadgyas for overseeing the production with great attention to detail and understanding.

Thank you Holly Alexander for expertly editing my recipes and to Xou Creative for making sense of it all through an articulated, less-is-more, great book design.

My most heartfelt thanks and love go to my husband, Chris, and our children, Louis and Anya. Chris' stamina, pursuit of excellence in his work and support of mine has made this book a reality. He's the truly original stand-up kind of guy and quietly supportive partner in life and work that makes my fulfilling world possible. While Louis and Anya balance it all and remind me that being a mother is the greatest gift of all.

THE SOUTHERN FORESTS
FOOD COUNCIL

The Southern Forests Food Council Inc. was founded in 2010 by a group of passionate local producers who recognised that the wealth and abundance of quality produce grown in the area provided the ideal platform to promote the region and foster a vibrant local economy and community for future generations.

Its role was formalised in 2012 after it received a $5 million investment under the State Government's SuperTowns initiative, with this investment being part of a $7 million Royalties for Regions allocation to the Shire of Manjimup for its Agricultural Expansion Project.

Ten local producers who, between them, have hundreds of years' experience in the industry, comprise the Council's Committee of Management.

The Food Council is committed to unifying the area's world-class and diverse producers to increase the value of agriculture, strengthen the region's economy, attract investment and export opportunities, promote regional pride, and create sustainable jobs.

It represents local producers, and culinary and agri-tourism operators who live and work in what is WA's premier food bowl. Its aim is to ultimately establish the Southern Forests region as an internationally recognised destination for outstanding produce and exceptional culinary tourism experiences.

The Southern Forests Food Council kindly supported the creation and publication of this book.

All enquiries about the images herein, by Craig Kinder of f22 Photography, can be directed to the Southern Forests Food Council via their website: www.southernforestsfood.com

BIBLIOGRAPHY

RECIPES

The Cook's Companion, Stephanie Alexander, Lantern, 2007.

Crazy Water, Pickled Lemons: Enchanting Dishes from the Middle East, Mediterranean and North Africa, Diana Henry, Mitchell Beazley, 2012.

Extra Virgin: Cooking with Olive Oil, Clare Ferguson, Ryland, Peters & Small, 2000.

Green Pickled Peaches: A Collection of Recipes and Memories, Chui Lee Luk, Hardie Grant, 2013.

The Kinfolk Table: Recipes for Small Gatherings, Nathan Williams, Artisan Division of Workman Publishing, 2013.

Maggie's Verjuice Cookbook, Maggie Beer, Lantern, 2012.

Maggie's Harvest, Maggie Beer, Lantern, 2008.

The Modern Pantry Cookbook, Anna Hansen, Ebury Press, 2012.

Mr Wilkinson's Favourite Vegetables: A Cookbook to Celebrate the Seasons, Matt Wilkinson, Murdoch Books, 2012.

Origin – The Food of Ben Shewry, Ben Shewry, Murdoch Books, 2013.

The River Cottage Meat Book, Hugh Fearnley-Whittingstall, Hodder & Stoughton, 2004.

Roo, Rabbit And Really Good Recipes, Doreen Owens, Moonya Aged Services, Manjimup.

TEXT

The Complete Book of Fruit Growing in Australia, Louis Glowinski, Hachette Australia, 2008.

The History, Landscape and Heritage of the Warren District, Christopher Berry, Shire of Manjimup, 1987.

Manjimup and the Warren District Past and Present, John Steward, Express Print, Bunburry, 2008.

Pioneering in the Karri Country, Dave Evans.

Southern Sketches: A tale of the development of the Warren & nearby districts, H.P. Evans, Department of Agriculture, 1993.

INDEX